Contract Negotiation Handbook
Software as a Service

Stephen Guth

This book is dedicated to you know who.

First Edition

Copyright © 2013 Stephen Guth

DISCLAIMER: THIS BOOK, ITS CONTENTS, AND THE INCLUDED CONTRACT TEMPLATE SHOULD IN NO WAY BE CONSTRUED AS A SUBSTITUTE FOR LEGAL ADVICE. READERS ARE ENCOURAGED TO SEEK COMPETENT LEGAL ADVICE REGARDING CONTRACTS AND OTHER LEGAL MATTERS RELATING TO "SOFTWARE AS A SERVICE" OR CLOUD COMPUTING CONTRACTING.

Published by Guth Ventures LLC, Alexandria, Virginia.

ISBN: 978-0-9888308-0-6

Library of Congress Control Number: 2013900041

Printed in the United States of America

10 9 8 7 6 5 4 3 2 1

About the Author

Stephen Guth is a legal and supply management professional with over 15-years of experience. He is a graduate of the University of Miami School of Law (J.D.), University of Maryland University College (M.S.M.), and Saint Leo University (B.A., summa cum laude). He is a Certified Professional in Supply Management and a Certified Commercial Contract Manager. Stephen is the author of *The Contract Negotiation Handbook: An Indispensable Guide for Contract Professionals*, *The Vendor Management Office: Unleashing the Power of Strategic Sourcing*, *Project Procurement Management: A Guide to Structured Procurements*, and *Hotel Contract Negotiation Tips, Tricks, and Traps*. Stephen is also the moderator of a blog that focuses on supply management, procurement, contracting, and vendor management topics (www.stephenguth.com).

Contents at a Glance

Table of Contents

Introduction

As a legal and supply management professional, I've always been amazed—perhaps astonished would be a more apt description—with how information technology (IT) goods and services are acquired. To provide an illustrative example, assume that your company decides it's going to build a small office building, about $7 million dollars in cost. In many ways, that's very similar to implementing an enterprise software system, like SAP or Oracle—where you're going to pay about the same amount in software license fees, implementation costs (external and internal resources), maintenance and support, training, and the like. For now, let's focus on your new office building...just imagine the people and processes that would be involved. You'll need an architect to flesh out your requirements right down to the last square foot. You'll also need a space planner to design the interior. You'll need site plans, floor plans, and engineering drawings. Of course, all of this needs to be within code and approved by various inspectors. All of the plans and drawings will be an attachment to the future contract with the builder. You'll select a builder through a rigorous competitive bidding process and likely develop a contract with very, very detailed requirements and detailed payment schedules (with holdbacks and liquidated damages). All parties involved will spend a significant amount of time negotiating a lengthy, robust contract. The good news is that, as is customary with commercial buildings, the parties will use an industry-standard contract template from the American Institute of Architects as a base for their written contract. During construction, there's intense day-by-day project and budget management. Change orders are clearly documented and nothing happens unless both parties are engaged and in agreement. Inspectors come and go, and where inspections reveal deficiencies, the builder is under intense scrutiny to fix them as soon as possible; otherwise, not much else can move forward. Finally, when the building is at completion, there's a punch list that the builder must complete before the building is accepted and you receive your certificate of occupancy. Imagine the detailed contract documents and other documents that paper all of this.

Even if you've never contracted for office construction services before, you may be familiar with how detailed and intense the procurement and contract management process is if you've ever had a house built.

Now compare that process with a typical software license procurement for an enterprise system like SAP or Oracle. In most cases, your stakeholders' requirements will be ill defined, so the resulting competitive bid isn't very substantial: it's a rushed process because your stakeholders want to get the project started as soon as possible. The prospective software vendors' sales representatives may be running amuck during the competitive bidding process, influencing your stakeholders. The software vendor that you ultimately select wants to do the deal using its contract template, which doesn't seem very comprehensive—but does seem very one-sided. The implementation services are also ill defined and are time and materials based (not deliverables based). For the license agreement and the accompanying services agreement, the software vendor doesn't want to commit to much of anything. In fact, the software vendor expressly disclaims even remotely possible Uniform Commercial Code (UCC) implied warranties and the software vendor's contract explicitly states that it doesn't guarantee the software will even work. The software vendor howls about revenue recognition when you want milestone payment holdbacks, service levels, and liquidated damages for non-performance. The software vendor doesn't want to give on acceptance periods and wants you to basically take the software as-is. During implementation, project management on the software vendor's side is spotty. Change orders are typically verbal and rarely documented. Scope creep and budget overruns become major issues. Both the stakeholders and the software vendor try to get the system slammed in so they can declare success. The end users, however, are bent out of shape when the system is finally delivered because it's lacking in the functionality that was promised. Hey, at least the software is up and running—which is a lot more than can be said for other software projects at your company.

So why is the process between procuring construction services and software so different? Particularly, when the process of "constructing" a building and "constructing" a software system is quite similar?

It boils down to process rigor. People just accept that the procurement and contracting of construction services is going to be a detailed and very thorough process. Imagine a builder not agreeing in its contract that the building it constructs will habitable. That builder would quickly go out of business because that position would be unacceptable to customers. However, that's what many software license agreements essentially state—software vendors don't agree that their software will meet your needs (software vendors typically disclaim the UCC implied warranty of fitness for particular purpose) or even work. Nevertheless, no one takes an issue with that as he or she would with a builder.

When it comes to IT procurements, money doesn't seem to be as much of an issue as with other goods or services, and users pretty much get whatever they think they want, price and terms and conditions be damned. Generally, the fine print and legalese of an IT contract isn't nearly as interesting as the new whiz-bang technology—until some issue with the vendor comes around to bite someone (usually *not* the vendor). Then the contract suddenly becomes all-important, typically too little and too late.

The lack of business discipline common to IT procurements is even more pervasive with the ever-growing popularity of software as a service (SaaS). That increasing pervasiveness is mostly due to SaaS service providers' sales representatives intentionally targeting end users and then those end users directly contracting with service providers while excluding IT and procurement departments. As a result, even though the risks are greater with cloud computing, there is even less business prudence and discipline with SaaS procurements than the already low degree of prudence and discipline with IT procurements generally.

In a broad sense, software can be either on-premises as with traditional software licenses or off-premises as with application service providers (single tenant) or SaaS service providers (multi-tenancy). As it relates to software / infrastructure / platform as a service, Gartner defines such offerings as "a style of computing where scalable and elastic IT-related capabilities are provided 'as a service' to customers using Internet technologies." Another way of looking at it is that SaaS, in essence, is the virtualization of on-premises software in a shared use environment. Consequently, contracts for SaaS are similar to traditional software license agreements albeit with some important differences in the form of unique and very real risks.

The first risk is perception-based. One selling point of SaaS is that an end user can bypass his or her IT department because, with SaaS, IT usually doesn't need to be involved. At least that's what the end user is made to believe by the service provider's sales representative. Another department that is frequently bypassed in the SaaS world is procurement because the end user is made to believe (again, by the sales representative) that he or she is buying functionality, not a license or other intellectual property rights as with traditional software procurements. While IT may or may not need to be involved, the user perception that functionality, and not rights, is being acquired is a risk-intensive disconnect between end users and procurement professionals. Frequently, a procurement department is engaged "after the fact" by an end user when something goes awry with the SaaS or the service provider—at which point the procurement department can do little to help.

Other real risks include, for example, the loss of access to SaaS (and the data) due to all sorts of service provider financial and legal calamities ranging from insolvency to insufficient business continuity planning to deteriorating business relationships with critical third-parties. Data corruption or loss due to poor service provider information security practices or other causes is another significant and tangible risk. Under a traditional software license where the licensor has given you a copy of its object code to install on your infrastructure and then occasionally patches the software, if the licensor goes belly up you may not have any immediate concerns—the software still runs (for a while). Not so with a SaaS service provider. The service provider has many more single points of failure and those failures, if they occur, will likely immediately impact subscribers. What happens if the service provider has a fire? What happens if the service provider's electricity is shut off for non-payment? What happens if the service provider needs more computing capacity for its infrastructure but doesn't have the capital or credit to obtain it? Some of these concerns can be addressed through your due diligence and other concerns can be addressed through a comprehensive and robust contract.

Keep in mind that service providers sell their SaaS offerings and related services day in and day out—they're experts at selling and getting the best possible deal for themselves and their shareholders. A subscriber (you) clearly doesn't acquire SaaS as frequently as a service provider sells the service, so that puts a subscriber (you) at a knowledge deficit, and, therefore, at a negotiation disadvantage.

Hence, this book: it addresses the risk-based concerns I've described and is intended to help a person representing a subscriber (that person is referred to as the "subscriber" or "you" throughout this book), such as a procurement professional or an attorney, to level the playing field and negotiate a fair and reasonable contract with a service provider. While I don't advocate that you overreach and try to squeeze every last penny of profit from a service provider, I do advocate your being prepared and educated in your negotiations with a service provider. And that's what this book is about—to help you (as the subscriber) get a fair deal. To achieve that goal, I'll deconstruct a SaaS contract section-by-section and provision-by-provision in this book. For key provisions, I'll describe and explain any negotiation tips, tricks, and traps you need to be aware of. Since it's helpful in any negotiation to put yourself in the shoes of the party you're negotiating with, where appropriate, I'll include what I think the position of a service provider might be.

The contract template that I'll be deconstructing and reviewing is what I call the "Master Software as a Service Agreement" or "SaaS Agreement." This book isn't an academic guide or legal treatise on contracts—it's a practical, *how-to* guide and it assumes some basic understanding of IT and IT contracting. I won't cover common contract provisions such as *No Waiver* and *Notices* (which are included in the SaaS Agreement) or contract basics such as what creates a binding contract. Even if you don't have any IT or IT contracting experience, you'll at least be in a better negotiation position by reading this book than if you were to try to go it alone and head-to-head with a service provider's sales or legal representative.

In my career thus far, I've negotiated, either directly or through my staff, thousands of contracts representing billions of dollars in spend. A majority of that was for IT goods and services. I've experienced gut-wrenching situations such as vendors failing to perform, vendors going belly up, "death by change order," and lawsuits due to contract disputes. In other words, I've seen it all. I've seen the best and worst of vendors and contracts. This book offers my unvarnished opinions as they relate to negotiating and contracting with SaaS service providers, with some readers certain to take exception to some part of what I've written in this book: use what makes sense for you and what you ethically feel comfortable with using.

Despite some of the tough positions I occasionally recommend that you take in this book or some of the shots that I take at service providers in describing their positions, I suggest being fair and reasonable. You want to get a fair deal, you want a relationship based on mutual commitment (as demonstrated by a solid, written contract), and you want the service provider to make a reasonable profit. Ultimately, you just want to get what you paid for. All of that is best accomplished by being fair and reasonable—and tough. So, let's get started...

Using Your Contract Template

The first step to a successful SaaS contract negotiation is to win the "battle of the forms." In other words, you need to ensure that *your* contract template (i.e., the SaaS Agreement) is used as the basis for negotiation and not the service provider's contract template. What's a contract template? It means the form of the agreement that is used by the parties to document the business relationship, obligations, responsibilities, rights, and remedies. A commonly used slang term for contract template is "paper," such as the service provider's "paper" or your "paper." The party that has drafted a contract template invariably constructs the template in such a way that it's more favorable to that party and shifts more obligations, limitations, liabilities, and risks to the other party. Thus, a service provider's contract template is obviously going to be more favorable to the service provider and less favorable to you.

Not only is the service provider's contract template going to be more favorable to the service provider, it also puts you in the difficult position of negotiating from the position of unfavorable to a less unfavorable or, at best, a neutral position—forget about ever getting to a favorable position. Unless you have a lot of leverage, you're going to have to work very hard to negotiate from the bottom up and the service provider is going to create this aura that it has already caved on so many language changes and concessions that you've already asked for. The net result is that the service provider is going to tire you out mid-way through the discussion of your redlines and you'll be more likely than not to start caving. For example, limitation of liability clauses are almost universally mutual and that's a given. Despite that, your service provider's contract template is likely to have a unilateral limitation of liability provision, limiting its liability and not limiting yours. You'll have to redline it to make it mutual, and then spend energy trying to negotiate your change because you can bet that the service provider isn't going to accept your redlines unchallenged. Instead, the service provider is going to drag out the negotiation and make you feel like it gave you a concession when the service provider finally agrees, if it does agree, to make the provision mutual—when the provision should have been that way to begin with. Then, you'll be incrementally fatigued and imbued with the feeling like you "owe the service provider one" because the service provider eventually gave into your redline. Good luck on the next change… A great way to get out of this trap is to have your own contract template.

Another efficiency of using your own contract template is that you have an intimate knowledge of it. You know what you can give on and what you really don't want to give on. You know of any tricks and traps that you've built into your contract template. Just like home games and being on home team turf, you have an inherent advantage in using your own contract template. It's also mentally exhausting to do a thorough job of redlining a service provider's contract template and it takes a fair amount of time. Shift those burdens to the service provider by using your own contract template.

Keep in mind that if you ever find yourself in a contract dispute where the issue is one of ambiguity of a contract term or condition, the court will interpret the contract against the drafter. That means, if you drafted a cruddy contract, it may come back to haunt you. However, just because courts interpret contracts in that way doesn't mean you shouldn't use your own contract template—it just means that you need to carefully draft the contract language your contract template contains.

Getting Leverage to Use "Your Paper"

Now that you're sold on using your own contract template, you'll have to overcome the hurdle of getting the service provider to use it. Sellers generally loathe using a buyer's contract template, but SaaS service providers are particularly adverse to the idea. By its very nature, SaaS is a pre-existing service and service providers therefore have pre-existing business parameters. That includes a business parameter of *standardization* (versus custom "one offs") as a means to reduce costs. That mentality permeates through nearly all business activities of a SaaS service provider, including its contracting practices. By having a standard contract template—and by forcing subscribers to use it—a service provider is able to reduce its cost of contracting. Consequently, service providers don't want to use a subscriber's contract template nor do service providers want to manage many different variations (due to subscriber redlines) of their own contract template. Some service providers want to use their contract template because it gives them flexibility that they otherwise wouldn't have, for example, by including hyperlinks to websites that describe contract terms and conditions or related subject matter such as service levels. It's a research-proven fact that service providers update hyperlinked contract terms and conditions frequently and with little or no notice.

The service providers' strong desire to use their contract templates hasn't yet become a complete reality. Despite the near certainty that you'll experience pushback from a service provider to use your contract template, according to industry research, roughly 50% of subscribers either used their own contract template or were able to negotiate substantive changes to a service provider's contract template. To be a part of that successful 50%, you need leverage to get a service provider to the negotiation table in terms of using your contract template. The brightest window of opportunity for you to use your contract template (or to at least make clear what contract provisions are particularly critical to you) is during the service provider selection or evaluation stages of a SaaS procurement. That's when your negotiation leverage is at its highest. The stages of selection or evaluation imply an important point; namely, that a competitive bid *is* being conducted (meaning a request for proposal or some other bid solicitation). If not, and your internal stakeholder comes to you with the service provider's contract template in hand and the need to do the deal as soon as possible (because all of the great discounts and incentives are going to end this Friday), you're likely stuck using the service provider's contract template. In that case, you'll be fighting tooth and nail to negotiate barely favorable terms and conditions. If you manage to get anything negotiated, consider yourself a hero.

Hopefully, you're out in front of upcoming deals and you have good relationships with your internal stakeholders such that your

SaaS procurement was competitively bid. That helps to get you to the right point of time where you can maximize your leverage, but you could let your leverage pass you by if you don't follow the right sequence of events. Specifically: (a) you must include the SaaS Agreement in the body of your bid solicitation (e.g., a request for proposal); (b) you must specify that the service provider is to redline or accept the SaaS Agreement as-is and, if redlined, to include the redlined version as a part of the service provider's proposal; and, (c) you must specify in your bid solicitation that the service provider's failure to redline or accept the SaaS Agreement as-is may result in immediate disqualification from the competitive bidding process and from further consideration. Something to the effect of the following in your bid solicitation would be helpful in achieving the desired result:

> The contract terms shall be defined by a written agreement that is not binding until fully executed by both parties. A copy of [Your Company]'s contract template is included as a part of this bid solicitation. Where Respondent does not currently have a written agreement with [Your Company], Respondent must submit, as part of its response to this bid solicitation, either an express acceptance of [Your Company]'s contract template without changes or specific contract language changes to [Your Company]'s contract template in the form of redlines. Failure to indicate such acceptance or to provide redlines may result in immediate disqualification and further consideration from the bid solicitation. While [Your Company] can show reasonable flexibility in contract terms and conditions, other factors being equal, preference will be given to Respondents who accept [Your Company]'s contract template without changes or take minimum exceptions.

Pre-Negotiations

Most of the ploys (what sellers use) and tactics (what buyers—you—use) in this book are rendered useless or unnecessary by "pre-negotiations," which is a tactic in itself. Unfortunately, you can only take advantage of the pre-negotiation tactic during a competitive bidding process—which is one more of many reasons why deals should be competitively bid as much as possible. In a competitive bid, such as for a SaaS procurement, pre-negotiations occur during the period of time between the receipt of service providers' bids and the final contract award.

When you think of the negotiation process in the context of procurement, you might think of a service provider and subscriber happily working together to conclude an agreement. In that context, however, the service provider infers that it's the chosen vendor and that the details of the deal just need to be worked out. If that's the case—the service provider believes or knows that it's the chosen vendor—a more accurate description of that working together isn't the subscriber negotiating with the service provider—it's called "begging." Here's why...

In a traditional competitive bid, the buyer receives the bids, evaluates the bids, eliminates all but the best proposal, and then begins negotiations with the finalist seller. At that point, the chosen seller assumes, and probably correctly, that the other sellers have been eliminated and possibly notified of their non-selection. In other words, the seller's competition has actually been eliminated by the buyer and the seller didn't even need to work at it. If the seller is shrewd, it will drag out the negotiations, seeking to create a length of time from the point of the finalist selection. In doing so, the seller causes the buyer to make a time investment in that seller which makes going back to a previously non-selected seller that much more difficult. After a while, the buyer has a vested interest in bringing the deal to a close and, if the seller is opportunistic, the buyer will leave a large sum of money and concessions on the table. That's why it's called begging instead of negotiating.

A better strategy is to create a short list of sellers and select two or more finalist sellers to "pre-negotiate" with before making a contract award. Sellers should be made aware of the fact that there are other sellers still in the mix and that the remaining sellers are being asked to provide "best and final offers" or "BAFOs." When a deal is agreed-upon and the contract is ready for signature, and only then, the contract is awarded and the finalist seller is announced.

This pre-negotiation process, along with including the SaaS Agreement as a part of your competitive bid, is the process that will provide you with the greatest leverage, get you the best deal, and get you onto your contract template.

Master Agreement / Exhibit Structure

Before delving into deconstructing the SaaS Agreement and dissecting its provisions, it's important to understand the general structure of the SaaS Agreement. The SaaS Agreement is one overall agreement, but it contains two separate components: the master agreement component and the exhibit component. The master agreement component contains all of the legal terms and conditions and "unless otherwise specified" language. Think of the master agreement component as the "legalese." As explained in the following paragraphs, the "unless otherwise specified" language provides the flexibility for the SaaS Agreement to be used repeatedly with the same service provider. The other component, the exhibit (called an "Exhibit A"), contains the business terms and describes a specific scope of services.

The master agreement component of the SaaS Agreement is a perpetual contract, so it never terminates unless one of the parties terminates it. That gives you the ability to use the SaaS Agreement to contract for a specific scope of services and then, any time later, contract for additional or different services (via another Exhibit A) without having to negotiate another contract. As opposed to the perpetual duration of the master agreement component, the scope of services contained in an Exhibit A does have a finite duration.

It's not uncommon for a subscriber to enter into an agreement with a service provider for a specific scope of services, and at some later point in time, subscribe to additional services. The benefit of the master agreement / exhibit structure is that the legalese is negotiated once. What if you want additional services distinct and separate from what you originally subscribed? With this structure, there's no need to do anything with the master agreement. No need to re-hash all of the legal terms and conditions with the accompanying arguing, debating, and hand wringing. You simply need to define the new scope of services with the service provider and write-up another Exhibit A.

If you do use the service provider again—and you didn't use a master agreement / exhibit structure the first time—you'll need to negotiate another contract. Typically, a fair amount of time is spent negotiating a fair and balanced contract with a service provider. As a part of that process, a fair amount of time is spent educating the service provider on what constitutes *reasonable* contract terms and conditions. More often than not, the service provider's representative, who you likely spent time educating and negotiating with, isn't there the next time you need to contract for more or new services. Even if you are negotiating with the same person, he or she may not be as agreeable on terms and conditions during a subsequent negotiation. For a number of reasons you're too polite to say aloud, you probably don't want to go through that same (usually arduous) education and negotiation process again. For all of these reasons— time, efficiency, and favorable terms and conditions—you'll likely prefer using a master agreement / exhibit structure which you can use repeatedly without much effort.

In order for the master agreement / exhibit structure to work well and be efficient, the master agreement needs to be flexible. As an example, the master agreement component of the SaaS Agreement contains an *Authorized Users; Authorized Uses* provision that defines who constitutes users that can use the services. It's in your best interest to ensure that the definition is as broad as possible. Thus, the *Authorized Users; Authorized Uses* provision in the SaaS Agreement broadly encompasses anyone who you want to use the services. If you're contracting for SaaS that has a sizeable fee associated with it, the service provider may be agreeable to such a broad definition of authorized users. On the other hand, if the fee isn't sizeable enough to dazzle the service provider, the service provider may not be agreeable to anything more than a limited and narrow definition of authorized users. That's where the magic "unless otherwise specified" language referenced earlier comes into play. Where certain deal points, such as authorized users, may be subject to change based on the specifics of the services being contracted for, the master agreement component contains language that permits its modification by the exhibit component. The magic language in the SaaS Agreement is typically found in the form of "Unless otherwise specified in an Exhibit A…" or something to that effect. This simple phrasing gives you a tremendous amount of flexibility and alleviates you from having to write all sorts of amendments and addendums to the SaaS Agreement as needs change and specific situations dictate. Here's the authorized users example with the magic language at the start of the provision:

1.1   <u>Authorized Users; Authorized Uses</u>. Unless otherwise limited on an <u>Exhibit A</u>, Service Provider grants Subscriber a renewable, irrevocable (unless as provided for herein), nonexclusive, royalty-free, and worldwide right for any Subscriber employee, contractor, or agent, or any other individual or entity authorized by Subscriber, (each, an "Authorized User") to access and use the Services. Other than those limitations expressly described in an <u>Exhibit A</u>, Authorized Users will have no other limitations on their access or use of the Services.

Where you don't have a large enough spend to warrant the broad description as provided for in the above provision, instead of amending the language from the master agreement component to something different, you can indicate to the service provider that the exhibit component permits the description to be modified by referring to the "Unless otherwise..." phrase. The broad definition is only the default, and is easily changed by specifying otherwise in the exhibit component. When a service provider pushes back on the default description contained in the master agreement component, you can respond that there could be additional spend on the horizon, and you can just specify a more narrow definition of authorized users in the exhibit component for the current scope of services. Usually the service provider buys into this, and, inevitably, forgets about the default (broad) definition of authorized user if and when an additional scope of services (another Exhibit A) is being negotiated.

Master Software as a Service Agreement

In this section, the SaaS Agreement is deconstructed and examined provision-by-provision. The general format of this deconstruction is the explanation of a contract provision immediately followed by the actual contract provision excerpted from the SaaS Agreement. To better tie specific explanations in the text to specific parts of the corresponding contract language in a provision, a number (e.g., [1]) is used to link the explanation to the corresponding provision. Non-critical provisions—those that are standard, boilerplate, or relatively innocuous—won't have much or any commentary. The SaaS Agreement is contained in *Appendix I ~ Master Software as a Service Agreement* in its entirety. Any [bracketed words] within the body of the SaaS Agreement are intended to be completed or tailored by the user of the SaaS Agreement (you).

If there are defined terms used in the provisions (a capitalized word or phrase is likely a defined term) for which the meaning isn't immediately obvious, *Appendix II ~ Defined Terms* will describe what the defined term refers to.

Assumptions

A contract for SaaS can be structured in any one of many different ways, with the structure usually being what optimizes ease of business and revenue for the service provider. Despite the many variations, a contract for SaaS is generally derived from one of three broad subscription metric types: user, hardware, or business transaction. The most common, by far, is the user metric. That metric typically involves authorized users, named users, concurrent users, user accounts, or role-based users. The next common is the hardware metric, which can include device / server, CPU / socket, host / node, or core / thread. The least common, and probably the most dubious (in that the metric is highly service provider-centric), is the business transaction metric that measures, for example, transactions such as manufacturing outputs, assets under management, revenue, or profit.

The SaaS Agreement contained in this book was drafted considering the following assumptions: a public cloud, a multi-tenant environment with a tenant-shared infrastructure, a per-user user subscription metric, scalable and elastic pricing using "tiers" of users, the highest classification of subscriber data is "personally identifiable information," and the services and data are based in the continental U.S.

Issue Spotting

There are a number of provisions in the SaaS Agreement, such as the *Subcontractors* provision, that a service provider will most certainly take issue with. In some cases, provisions are intentionally structured to trigger an issue with a service provider. For example, in the *Representations and Warranties* section, an included warranty states that the service provider will never withhold any services when you're reasonably disputing a fee. This language was included in part because less-than-scrupulous service providers have been holding a subscriber's data hostage when there was a payment dispute. If a service provider was to take issue with that warranty—or any other provision related to withholding services or the extraction of your data—it's a golden opportunity for you to "spot the issue," conduct additional due diligence, and make informed decisions.

It's no surprise that a major driver to the cloud is cost reduction; however, many of the anticipated costs savings that subscribers expect are not achieved due to hidden costs. These hidden costs include fees for such things as pilots, initial setup, initial training and recurring training, customization and integration, development and test (i.e., sandbox) environments, data storage, data extraction, non-traditional users (e.g., public, business partners, suppliers), and termination transition services. In the SaaS Agreement, the services fees are characterized as "all-in." Other fees not a part of the all-in services fees are specifically called-out and described, and, where appropriate, other obligations of the service provider are designated to be without charge or additional cost. These characterizations and designations will also help you to spot issues in terms of hidden costs because the service provider will be forced to take exception to language where the service provider anticipates hitting you with a cost.

Preamble, Recitals, and Words of Agreement

The first part of the SaaS Agreement—and, for that matter, any well drafted contract—contains the [1] preamble, [2] recitals, and [3] words of agreement.

[1] The preamble contains basic information about the contract, such as the name of the agreement, the date that the agreement is to be effective, and the names and addresses of the parties. Some consider the preamble and recitals to be one and the same, and refer to both collectively as the "preamble."

[2] The recitals, sometimes referred to as the "preamble" or "whereas clauses," aren't really terms and conditions of the contract (as explained in the discussion of the "words of agreement" in the following paragraph). Instead, the recitals serve to explain the purpose of the contract and the intent of the parties in a relatively brief format. Some believe that recitals are unnecessary legalese, but, when drafted correctly, recitals are an easy way to gain an understanding of the contract before (and instead of) having to read through all of the fine print. In addition to telling the story of the contract, the recitals in a buyer-seller contract provide a forum for describing why the buyer depends and relies on the seller to perform. Doing so aids in developing detrimental reliance: if the seller doesn't perform exceptionally—as stated in the recitals—the buyer might be damaged.

This dependence and reliance may be extremely helpful if a subscriber is trying to show in a subsequent dispute that it went through a thoughtful process in selecting the service provider and relied on the service provider in meeting the needs of the subscriber. That's exactly what's accomplished in the recitals below: that the subscriber needed a service provider that's in the business of providing SaaS (first whereas), that the subscriber conducted due diligence by requesting a proposal from the service provider (second whereas), that the service provider has the requisite experience and expertise in providing SaaS (third whereas), that the service provider, with all of its experience and expertise, submitted a proposal to the subscriber describing the SaaS required by the subscriber (fourth whereas), that the subscriber selected the service provider to provide the SaaS because of the service provider's experience and expertise (fifth whereas), that the service provider wants to provide the SaaS to the subscriber and that the service provider knows how important its performance is to the subscriber (sixth whereas), and that the service provider is fully aware of the terms and conditions under which it is to provide the SaaS (seventh whereas).

It should be obvious to a reader of the recitals where the story leads: if the service provider screws up, it was aware of the impact of its screw-up, and it had better make good. You should modify the recitals to meet your specific situation, but it's recommended that you follow the same logical, step-by-step format, culminating in the service provider acknowledging that it does in fact want to provide the services that you are contracting for. If a service provider doesn't want you to include any recitals, or the service provider significantly modifies the recitals such that they're watered-down, the obvious question that should be raised is "why?" If the service provider is adamant about its deletion or changes, it may be appropriate to give up on the recitals as a concession or as a trade for some other provision that's more valuable to you. However, you should ensure that any changes the service provider makes to the recitals doesn't put any potential liability or burden back on you.

[3] The words of agreement are a formality, used to signify that the parties are expressly agreeing to all of the following terms and conditions, and that the parties have exchanged "consideration." Consideration is a necessary element of the three most basic elements of contract formation in the U.S. (offer, acceptance, consideration). Consideration is anything of value—it doesn't *have* to be money—promised to another when making a contract. In the context of the SaaS Agreement, the consideration is your paying one or more types of fees for the service provider's services and the service provider promising to provide the services. Everything

before the words of agreement, such as the recitals, does *not* have contractual force, but everything after does.

[1]MASTER SOFTWARE AS A SERVICE AGREEMENT

This agreement ("Agreement") is entered into, to be effective as of [Effective Date] ("Effective Date"), by and between **[SUBSCRIBER NAME]** located at [Subscriber Address] ("Subscriber") and **[SERVICE PROVIDER NAME]** located at [Service Provider Address] ("Service Provider").

[2]RECITALS

WHEREAS, Subscriber requires third-party hosted "software as a service" (the "Services," as further described herein) with respect to certain of its information technology needs;

WHEREAS, Subscriber requested a proposal from Service Provider for such Services;

WHEREAS, Service Provider has experience and expertise in the business of providing the Services;

WHEREAS, Service Provider submitted a proposal to Subscriber to perform such Services on behalf of Subscriber;

WHEREAS, based on Service Provider's superior knowledge and experience relating to such Services, Subscriber has selected Service Provider to provide and manage the Services;

WHEREAS, Service Provider wishes to perform the Services and acknowledges that the successful performance of the Services and the security and availability of Subscriber's data ("Subscriber Data," as further described herein) are critical to the operation of Subscriber's business; and,

WHEREAS, Service Provider has agreed to provide the Services to Subscriber, all on the terms and conditions set forth herein.

[3]NOW, THEREFORE, in consideration of the mutual covenants and representations set forth in this Agreement, the parties hereby agree as follows:

The Services

This section starts by summarizing the services and by [1] enumerating a list of services to be provided by the service provider. However, since there's an inherent risk in using lists as something might be forgotten or not thought of at the time the list was created, the list is purposely not all-inclusive and is only meant for illustrative purposes. Hence, the term "including" that precedes the list. Service providers may object to some of the services enumerated in the list, which is the primary purpose of the list: it may be that you thought the service provider was to provide something that ultimately it didn't plan on providing (at least, not as a part of the base services fees). What a service provider includes as a part of the services may be murky when discussing the subject at a demo or a sales meeting, but, interestingly, a high degree of clarity as to what's included or not included arises when a service provider is faced with actual contract language. Any objections by the service provider to this list will be your opportunity to have a scope of services discussion with the service provider. To cast a wide net, the language of the section [2] defines services to include anything necessary to make productive use of the services. Again, this is another opportunity to have the scope of services discussion should the service provider object to this language. Ideally, a service provider will not object to any of the foregoing. You can then rest assured that the service provider will be obligated to do what is necessary to enable the use of the services and that little, if anything, will ever fall out of scope.

For reasons further described in the *Acknowledgement of License Grant* provision, the [3] services are characterized as a license grant of hosted software.

This section also sets-up and describes the mechanics of the master agreement / exhibit structure. [4] Each different scope of services (or module thereof) to be provided by the service provider under the SaaS Agreement becomes a different exhibit (Exhibit A), and each different exhibit is numbered accordingly (Exhibit A-1 for the first scope of services, Exhibit A-2 for the next scope of services, and so on). [5] The form of an Exhibit A is attached to the master agreement component for reference purposes only and to illustrate what the Exhibit A to the SaaS Agreement looks like. Therefore, the first time you execute the SaaS Agreement with a service provider and acquire the SaaS, the following contract documents will exist: the SaaS Agreement, Exhibit A (the form, for reference purposes only), and Exhibit A-1 (for the first scope of services). As explained earlier, if you decide to acquire any additional services offered by the service provider, only another Exhibit A needs to be created and executed (Exhibit A-2 in this example)—there is no need to negotiate and execute another SaaS Agreement.

In some cases, a service provider might provide you with a document that contains all of the information that an Exhibit A would contain. If, for whatever reason, it doesn't make sense for you to transfer all of that information into the format specified by the Exhibit A form, you have another option. This part of [6] the provision provides the option of a document not in the Exhibit A format to be used in place of that format. However, you should use the form of the Exhibit A as a checklist to ensure that the service provider's document covers everything that needs to be included. You must also ensure that the preamble from the Exhibit A form is copied and pasted to the beginning of the service provider's document and the signature block from the Exhibit A form is copied and pasted to the end of the service provider's document. Without the preamble included at the beginning of the service provider's document, the document won't be covered by the SaaS Agreement since it won't be contractually integrated. Keep in mind that using the service provider's document isn't optimal and perhaps a little sloppy because there are defined terms in the SaaS Agreement that aren't likely the same terms as used in the service provider's document.

At this point, it makes sense to describe what a defined term is and the process of defining a term. Sometimes a word or a phrase is used repeatedly in a contract. When that word or phrase has special meaning or emphasis attached to it, it should be defined on its first use (or it can be included in a definitions section at the beginning of a contract) and then all subsequent references to that word or phrase should be capitalized; for example, the word "Agreement." The word "Agreement" is capitalized because it was defined (in the preamble) and will be referred to elsewhere in the SaaS Agreement. Thus, whenever a subscriber uses "Agreement," the contract reader knows that the subscriber is referring to the SaaS Agreement that he or she is reading and not some other agreement.

1. __The Services__. This Agreement sets forth the terms and conditions under which [3]Service Provider agrees to license to Subscriber certain hosted software and provide [2]all other services necessary for productive use of such software [1]including customization / integration, user identification and password change management, data import / export, monitoring, technical support, maintenance, training, backup and recovery, and change management (the "Services") as [4]further set forth on an Exhibit A (sequentially numbered) [5]in the form of the Exhibit A attached hereto [6]or in other statements of services containing substantially similar information and identified as an Exhibit A. The Agreement shall remain in effect unless terminated as provided for herein.

Authorized Users; Authorized Uses

One of the most critical provisions in a software license is the description of who has the right to use the software—typically called the license grant. What legal entities have the right to use the software? Who's covered? Employees, contractors, outsourced service providers, suppliers, customers? Where, geographically, can the software be used? What are the limitations of use?

The goal of the licensor (the seller) as it relates to the software grant is to make the definition of user as narrow as possible so as to increase the possibility of additional revenue should the licensee (the buyer) need to add users. The goal of the licensee is exactly the opposite; rather, the licensee wants to cast as wide of a net as possible so as to avoid paying anything more than it already has for additional types of users. While not a software license agreement in the traditional sense, the provision describing who can use the software in the SaaS Agreement is just as critical. Whether a private cloud or public cloud implementation, you must carefully consider who really needs to use the services and ensure that whoever does need to use the services has the contractual right to do so.

The language of the *Authorized Users; Authorized Uses* provision does cast a wide net. In doing so, it uses some terms common to traditional software licensing. The [1] services are not irrevocable, meaning that they cannot be discontinued unless you have materially breached the SaaS Agreement (and fail to cure), the SaaS Agreement is terminated, or the associated Exhibit A is terminated or expires. In other words, the service provider doesn't have the ability to threaten discontinuation of the services as bargaining leverage without a basis permitted by the SaaS Agreement. The use of the SaaS is not geographically limited and can be used "worldwide," which means that the service provider cannot charge additional services fees if you require use of the services in a location not originally contemplated at the time the SaaS Agreement was executed. [2] In terms of authorized users, the scope couldn't be any greater. Not only are the typical users of employees, contractors, and agents included, any individual or entity that is authorized by you has the right to access and use the services. That gives you significant flexibility. If you're buying tiers (or "blocks") of users, a service provider likely won't object to the broad nature of this definition of authorized user—the more users that have the right to use the services, the better for the service provider (provided that you pay for the additional number of users). However, some service providers may object to the broad language because they somehow perceive it as a lost opportunity for additional revenue. For example, a service provider might charge a certain fee for a certain type of user in a tier or block (such as employees) and charge a higher fee for another type (such as suppliers). If a service provider objects to this broad nature of the language, it's critical to determine why and what the impact to you might be. Also, since [3] this provision is subject to modification by an Exhibit A via the magic language (i.e., "Unless otherwise limited on an Exhibit A..."), the preferred alternative to redlining the language in the body of the SaaS Agreement is to leave the provision as-is and instead amend it via the Exhibit A.

1.1   Authorized Users; Authorized Uses. Unless otherwise limited on an Exhibit A, [1]Service Provider grants Subscriber a renewable, irrevocable (unless as provided for herein), nonexclusive, royalty-free, and worldwide right for [2]any Subscriber employee, contractor, or agent, or any other individual or entity authorized by Subscriber, (each, an "Authorized User") to access and use the Services. [3]Other than those limitations expressly described in an Exhibit A, Authorized Users will have no other limitations on their access or use of the Services.

Acknowledgement of License Grant

With a traditional software license, the license is purchased by the licensee, the software is delivered by the licensor, and the software is installed on the licensee's technology infrastructure. In a sense, under that structure, the software is something tangible that is "possessed" by the licensee (subject to the terms of the license, of course). If the licensor declared bankruptcy and attempted to reject the license (meaning to terminate the licensee's right to use the software), Section 365(n) of the U.S. Bankruptcy Code allows the licensee to retain its right to the use of the intellectual property, i.e., the software. In contrast, SaaS can be viewed as a mere service delivered by a service provider—and not viewed as a license of a right to intellectual property. If that view of SaaS is accepted by a court, then Section 365(n) doesn't apply because it only applies to rights related to intellectual property. The result is that you would be left holding the bag if the service provider goes belly up: your money out the door and nothing to show for it.

To avoid that result and to position you to take advantage of Section 365(n), if necessary, and continue using the services (or at least the escrowed software; see the *Escrow Agreement* provision) should the service provider go belly up, the underlying concept of the SaaS Agreement is oriented toward a license of intellectual property versus a mere services agreement. For example, the SaaS Agreement contains provisions such as *Changes in Number of Authorized Users* and *Proprietary Rights Indemnification* that have elements consistent with a traditional software license. Further, the SaaS Agreement is peppered with the word "license" (or some derivation thereof) throughout. Among other things, these examples serve to demonstrate to a court that the SaaS Agreement is a license of a right to intellectual property. However, taking a "belt and suspenders" approach, the *Acknowledgement of License Grant* provision attempts to make the matter unambiguous—that, for the purposes of the Bankruptcy Code, the SaaS Agreement *is* a license grant. If your service provider takes issue with this provision, you may want to probe its financials more closely.

1.2   Acknowledgement of License Grant. For the purposes of 11 U.S.C. § 365(n), the parties acknowledge and agree that this Agreement constitutes a license grant of intellectual property in software form to Subscriber by Service Provider.

Changes in Number of Authorized Users

[1] Exhibit A is where the details are described for the initial number of authorized users and tiers or bands for acquiring additional authorized users. The *Changes in Number of Authorized Users* provision gives you the right to increase and decrease (subject to a minimum commitment) the number of authorized users. It's worth pointing out that "software as a service" can become "shelfware as a service" if the rollout of the SaaS Agreement is not fully thought out.

Industry publications have described SaaS implementations gone expensively awry where subscribers have acquired their full need of authorized users upon the execution of a SaaS Agreement and then took a year or more to rollout the service to users. In other words, many more users were acquired and paid-for than could be made immediately productive during the SaaS implementation. Some subscribers make that mistake because their rollout just wasn't thought through well enough and other subscribers are bedazzled by high volume discounts for their initial acquisition of authorized users. The best position for you to be in is to have a flexible SaaS Agreement that permits the acquisition of authorized users on a basis consistent with the speed at which your organization and users can digest the use of the service. The SaaS Agreement must accommodate that type of rollout and tiers of authorized users must be described in a manner by which you can acquire additional authorized users when you need them—that's what this provision does.

[2] The initial number of authorized users that you specify and pay for in the Exhibit A becomes your minimum commitment. Thus, consistent with the reasons described in the preceding paragraph, you should buy the lowest required number of authorized users considering a conservative rollout schedule. While you have the ability to adjust the number of authorized users, [3] you will always (unless otherwise agreed) be responsible for paying for the minimum commitment. The rationale for including that limitation, which isn't necessarily subscriber-friendly, is one of compromise. Allowing a subscriber to increase usage clearly doesn't present a dilemma to a service provider, but, in contrast, a service provider isn't particularly keen about its subscribers having the right to decrease usage. Hence, to bargain for your right to decrease the number of authorized users by some amount, a service provider needs something in return and that something is the expected revenue stream represented by a minimum commitment of authorized users. [4] Over time, either party may desire to change the minimum commitment. For example, a service provider may want it increased because you maintained a significantly higher

number of authorized users over the life of the relationship than what was originally contracted. If you subsequently elect to decrease usage to levels representative of those in the early years of the relationship, the level of revenue the service provider has come to expect would be severely diminished. On the other hand, you may not contract for much or any more usage over a period of time and, in fact, experience a waning need for the services. You may then desire a lower baseline of usage.

[5] To initiate an adjustment (other than an adjustment to the minimum commitment, which is not permitted), you must notify the service provider in writing. The adjustment that you do make must correspond to the tiers described in the Exhibit A, which, in turn, means that you should be very thoughtful at the time of contract negotiation about specifying the tiers to be contained in the Exhibit A and what works best (i.e., tighter tiers or broader tiers) in your environment. Following the request, the service provider has 5-business days to implement the adjustment. This expedited turn-around time facilitates your ability to wait until the last possible moment to increase usage (and pay additional fees) or, in the case of decreasing usage, not having to pay for usage you don't need.

1.3   Changes in Number of Authorized Users. [1]The Services are provided on a tiered basis, such tiers as further described in an Exhibit A. Subscriber agrees to license the [2]initial number of Authorized Users described in such Exhibit A (the "Minimum Commitment"). Subscriber is entitled to increase or decrease the number of Authorized Users on an as-requested basis; provided, however, that [3]Subscriber shall maintain the Minimum Commitment [4]unless the parties otherwise agree to adjust the Minimum Commitment. [5]Should Subscriber elect to change the number of Authorized Users, Service Provider shall reduce or increase Authorized Users to the corresponding tier described in the Exhibit A and adjust the prospective Services Fees accordingly no later than five (5) business days from Subscriber's written request.

Control and Location of Services

The *Control and Location of Services* section goes to who is in control of providing the services, who is performing the services, and where the services are being performed. **[1]** While who's in charge of performance is obvious on the surface (it's the service provider), it's helpful to make it clear in the SaaS Agreement for at least two reasons. One reason goes to reliance. It's the service provider, not you, who is in the business of providing the services and you're relying on the service provider's expertise. If the service provider doesn't perform the services in a manner consistent with sellers of similar services, you have a more robust claim for breach in the case of underperformance if the associated contract spells out your reliance on the service provider. There is a theme of reliance woven throughout the SaaS Agreement, most prominently in this section, the *Recitals* section, and the *Representations and Warranties – By Service Provider* provision. The other reason is a bit more esoteric and relates to the doctrine of impracticability. Under a buyer-seller contract, if the buyer exerts too much control over the seller and the seller subsequently underperforms, the seller could argue (under the doctrine of impracticability) that it shouldn't be held liable because of the buyer's control—had the buyer not controlled the seller, the seller could argue that it would have or could have satisfactorily performed the contract. To make clear who is responsible for specifying and performing the services (and to avoid the possibility of the foregoing argument of the service provider), the language of this provision explicitly states that the service provider is ultimately responsible but that the service provider will consider your requests in the course of performing the services.

Data is a widely covered concern under the SaaS Agreement, most notably, in the *Subscriber Data, Non-Disclosure of Confidential Information,* and *Data Privacy and Information Security* sections. How data is handled and protected is clearly critical, but, relative to privacy laws and regulations, so is the location of data. **[2]** The sole purpose of the location component of this section—which restricts all elements of the services including computing, communications, and data storage to the continental U.S.—is to avoid cross-border and foreign laws relating to data privacy as well as security concerns inherent with computing and data storage in locations outside of the continental U.S. Service providers, in a drive to improve margin by lowering costs, may use infrastructure and / or subcontractors outside of the continental U.S. Sometimes that isn't made entirely clear to prospective subscribers during the sales process—the language in this section will help to shed light (through a service provider's objection to the language) on exactly where the service provider's infrastructure is (and where your data will be). If the location of your data outside of the continental U.S. isn't just a matter of low cost convenience for the service provider and you have a need for the data to be located in a foreign jurisdiction (or you are located outside of the continental U.S.), then this component of the provision would need to be adjusted. Contract language may also need to be added to other sections and provisions, perhaps under the warranty of compliance with laws contained in the *Representations and Warranties – Mutual* provision, the *Data Privacy and Information Security* section, and the *Compliance with Laws; Subscriber Policies and Procedures* provision. This additional contract language should be drafted to ensure that the service provider is required to comply with appropriate international law (such as the European Union Data Retention Directive).

1.4 <u>Control and Location of Services</u>. [1]The method and means of providing the Services shall be under the exclusive control, management, and supervision of Service Provider, giving due consideration to the requests of Subscriber. Except as otherwise specified in an <u>Exhibit A</u>, [2]the Services (including data storage), shall be provided solely from within the continental United States and on computing and data storage devices residing therein.

Subcontractors

Service providers in the SaaS space—particularly new entrants—frequently rely on third-parties to provide some element of the services such as infrastructure or software components. Depending on your situation, a service provider's use of subcontractors may or may not be an issue; however, without knowing whether subcontractors will be used or not, you can't make an informed choice. If the use of subcontractors doesn't present an issue for you, you still want to ensure that the service provider is ultimately responsible for the services: you don't want the service provider pointing at a subcontractor and deflecting responsibility if a service level is missed or something else goes awry. You also don't want to have any obligation to pay subcontractors if the service provider doesn't. To ensure you're aware, [1] the service provider is not permitted the use of subcontractors or to otherwise make (through assignment or transfer) any third-party responsible for anything under the SaaS Agreement unless you specifically agree in writing. Some service providers will balk at this language. In an effort to get the language removed, they will tell you that they use subcontractors, there's no way around it, and that the language creates a burden on a service provider in that it needs to come to you for every little subcontract the service provider has in place or wants to put into place. Assuming that the use of subcontractors is not a problem in your situation, tell the service provider that it can include the names of those subcontractors in the corresponding Exhibit A for the services and that doing so will constitute your consent (for those subcontractors, not future ones). Also tell the service provider that it's important for you to be kept informed of who is involved in performing the services as you specifically selected the service provider (hopefully on the strength of the service provider's proposal that resulted from a competitive bid) to perform the services and not a legion of unknown others. It's reasonable for you to be informed and have a say. [2] If the service provider does subcontract or makes a third-party responsible for any aspect of the services, that act is void (and results in a material breach). In any case, [3] whether or not you agree to the use of subcontractors, the service provider is solely responsible for the performance of the services and other obligations under the SaaS Agreement. Ultimately, you want "one throat to choke" or, more optimistically, "a single person to hug."

1.4.1   Subcontractors.   [1]Service Provider shall not enter into any subcontracts for the performance of the Services, or assign or transfer any of its rights or obligations under this Agreement, without Subscriber's prior written consent and [2]any attempt to do so shall be void and without further effect and shall be a material breach of this Agreement. [3]Service Provider's use of subcontractors shall not relieve Service Provider of any of its duties or obligations under this Agreement.

Offensive or Disparaging Content

The good news is that SaaS, generally, results in a lower total cost when compared to traditional software licensing or software development. That lower cost is due to SaaS being a multi-tenancy model, where many other subscribers ("tenants") access the same (or parts of the same) infrastructure and therefore share in costs. The bad news is that SaaS is, well, a multi-tenancy model. That good news / bad news quip applies to every aspect of your data—you'll see that echoed throughout this book, particularly as it relates to privacy and security. It also applies to the environment in which your authorized users interact with your data. One example is a login portal: depending on the SaaS, every subscriber (not just you) goes through the same portal. With another SaaS, you may have a custom or "private" portal. What the *Offensive or Disparaging Content* provision is intended to address is the situation where other subscribers might come across something in the use of the services that disparages your company or your authorized users come across something that they feel is offensive.   Keep in mind a low threshold for what's offensive—even a mundane advertisement can be offensive merely because it's an advertisement.

The *Offensive or Disparaging Content* provision, particularly if you're more used to traditional software licensing, may strike you as odd or maybe even over-the-top and unnecessary. If so, consider this language excerpted from a service provider's SaaS contract template:

Subscriber understands that by using the Service, Subscriber may be exposed to Content that might be offensive, harmful, inaccurate, or otherwise inappropriate, and that Subscriber has no claim against Service Provider for any such material. Subscriber further understands that the Service may include advertisements or other content, which may be targeted to the Content or information on the Service, queries made through the Service, or other information, and Subscriber has no claim against Service Provider for the placement of advertising or similar content on the Service or in connection with the display of Content or information from the Service whether submitted by Subscriber or others.

If service providers are actively including language similar to the foregoing excerpt in their SaaS contract templates, which requires you to be okay with offensive content and gives you no rights whatsoever, then the *Offensive or Disparaging Content* provision probably isn't odd or over-the-top—and *is* necessary. However, a service provider may object to the language in this provision because it doesn't apply to its services or your particular situation. That sounds reasonable on its face, but what about the seemingly unrelated matter of your agreeing to an initial set of subcontractors providing services on behalf of the service provider? What happens if a subcontractor controls some element of the interface or the user experience? The point is that the contract language may not seem on its face to be applicable, but it may very well be. The best option is to negotiate to keep the language in. If offensive or disparaging content is never going to be an issue (according to the service provider), then the service provider shouldn't have to worry about the language being invoked.

[1] If the services, or any web services that are indirectly associated with the services, are found to contain any offensive content or content that disparages you, you'll have certain remedies. [2] The standard of determining whether content is offensive or disparaging is in your sole determination, not the service provider's determination. A service provider may request mutual determination or at its determination. An argument in response to that would be the subjectivity of the analysis, which can only be done by the

subscriber: it's not necessarily a bright line or binary analysis. The service provider doesn't have the same basis or context as do you. For example, if you work for a company that's in the business of selling broccoli, it's very possible that any content that extols the benefits of vitamin C supplements will be considered offensive. Because it's not a service provider's area of knowledge or expertise, the service provider might not agree with the connection that vitamin supplements, as a substitute for foodstuffs of nutritional value, impact the sale of vegetables and that the allegedly offensive content is indeed offensive. That might be an absurd example, but it serves to illustrate the subtle nature of the analysis and the need for it to be made in the subscriber's context.

Where you do find offensive or disparaging content, you have one specified remedy and then a choice of two additional remedies. [3] The first remedy is the immediate removal of the objectionable content. [4] The choice of additional remedies is between [5] terminating the services that the objectionable content is affiliated with and getting any prepaid fees returned or [6] continuing with the services and essentially getting the services for free for the then-current term (via prepaid fees returned to you or the extinguishment of any obligation to pay if you haven't already paid). Most service providers won't take issue with the obligation to remove the objectionable content but nearly all will take issue with the risk of your right to terminate the services and their possibility of giving up current revenue or losing future revenue. A reasonable alternative would be to forgo the right to terminate the services and to agree to some lesser amount of liquidated damages such as a month of fees waived.

1.4.2   Offensive or Disparaging Content. [1]Where the Services or any web services affiliated with the Services contain offensive content or portray Subscriber in a disparaging way, either [2]as solely determined by Subscriber, [3]Service Provider shall immediately remove the offensive or disparaging content and [4]Subscriber shall have the right, at Subscriber's sole election, to: [5](a) immediately terminate this Agreement or any Exhibit A corresponding to the offending or disparaging content and be entitled to a return of any prepaid fees, as liquidated damages and not as a penalty; or, [6](b) obtain or retain, as the case may be, all fees paid or payable for the entire period of the then-current term, as liquidated damages and not as a penalty, associated with any Exhibit A corresponding to the offending or disparaging content.

Storage

Storage in the context of SaaS is frequently, at the least, an afterthought, and, at the worst, a surprise. As many other mature industries have done or are doing, service providers are unbundling certain components of SaaS as additional revenue opportunities. Service providers have the same argument as do airlines, hotels, and other industries that have become wizards at coming up with new and innovative ways to zing customers with additional fees. Their argument is that they only want to make sure that whoever is consuming a service is paying for it and those who don't need the service aren't paying for it. That sounds nice, but somehow, nearly everyone gets to pay. For example, do people really have the option to opt out of the so-called "resort fee" at resorts? Service providers apply that same argument to storage: you only have to pay for what you use and, under the guise of "consumerism," you'll manage your storage appropriately so as to manage your costs.

Depending on your bargaining leverage or needs, you may be able to negotiate away any extra fees for storage and you therefore won't need the *Storage* provision, but, if you can't, the provision will at least help to eliminate the surprise factor that could occur when you need additional storage. Since the Exhibit A will [1] describe an initial amount of storage that could be exceeded at some point in the future, [2] the service provider is required to notify you when you're at 80% of your current capacity. That obligation to notify you when you reach that 80% threshold is a continuing one (hence, the "then-current" reference). There are horror stories where service providers only provided notice to subscribers when they hit 100% of their storage capacity and forced the subscribers to immediately buy additional storage at inflated prices. With an 80% threshold, you should have enough notice that you can perhaps purge data to delay the need to buy additional storage. [3] It's imperative that the Exhibit A contain pricing for any additional increases in storage capacity. Note that, over time, storage technology is cheaper to produce and has increasingly higher capacities: the reductions in storage costs can be dramatic. Similarly, your costs as described in an Exhibit A should reflect that. If the described storage costs increase over time or even stay flat, that's unreasonable and you should be able to forge a better bargain. A cost-plus model may make sense, where you agree to the "plus" to protect your service provider's margin as the "cost" decreases for the both of you over time. If a service provider doesn't agree, which has happened, with the historically proven fact that storage costs decrease over time, the service provider is either fabricating its own reality or is technologically ignorant (or both).

Other than the pricing, there is nothing particularly objectionable about this provision except in the case that a service provider doesn't have the ability to notify you "immediately" and wants more time. A few days might be reasonable, but, at the same time, you may then want to lower the threshold to 70% or some other percentage so as to give you ample time to either reduce usage or buy more capacity. A service provider may also take issue with having to provide the additional capacity within 5-calendar days due to the possible need to acquire more storage or for other legitimate reasons. Again, some extra time—but not too much—is a reasonable compromise.

1.5   Storage. The Services shall include [1]the applicable allocation of base data storage described in an Exhibit A. [2]Service Provider shall immediately notify Subscriber when Subscriber has reached eighty percent (80%) of Subscriber's then-current data storage maximum. Within five (5) calendar days of Subscriber's request, Service Provider shall make additional data storage available to Subscriber [3]at the rates described in the Exhibit A.

Development and Test Environments

With the SaaS model, the need for anything other than a production environment is uncommon. However, if the SaaS that you're acquiring is more sophisticated or niche than the typical garden-variety SaaS offering, it's possible you'll need a development environment and it's more likely you'll need a test environment. Since the premise behind SaaS is standardization, user-specific development or heavy customization is out of the norm. However, if your SaaS permits subscriber extensions or some other customization, you'll need both a development and test environment (the SaaS Agreement contemplates the need for subscriber customization; see the *Customization / Integration Services* provision). If the foregoing is not the case for you, you still may want a test environment in order to test service provider maintenance and enhancements before they're introduced into production (see the *Acceptance of Non-Emergency Maintenance* provision, which allows for subscriber testing of maintenance prior to elevation to production). Although these environments are more the exception than the norm, it's common for a service provider to want to charge for them when the environments are available to subscribers. Subscribers that do request (and receive) the right to test maintenance and enhancements are frequently chagrined to later discover that they failed to include the cost (or to negotiate it away) of a test environment.

This *Development and Test Environments* provision will likely raise a number of objections from a service provider. The first is that the environments are to be provided [1] without charge. The service provider may also want to [2] limit the data that you use to develop and test with to a subset so as to reduce its data storage costs. Similarly, the service provider likely [3] won't want to commit to the same computing capacity (meaning, speed of processing) that is available in the production environment. Further, the service provider may want to [4] add some specificity around what "requests" and "managing" means in terms of responsibilities and timing. Subject to your specific needs, these may be acceptable objections. It's possible that you could bargain for "no additional charge" provided that you limit your data storage requirements and have lower expectations for processing speed.

1.6   Development and Test Environments. In addition to production use of the Services, Subscriber is entitled to one development and one test environment for use by Authorized Users [1]at no additional charge.   Such non-production environments shall have the same [2]data storage and [3]processing capacities as the   production   environment.   Service   Provider   shall [4]cooperate with Subscriber's requests in managing the non-production environments such as refreshing Subscriber Data upon request.

Documentation

The purpose of documentation for the services is to [1] adequately describe the functions and features of the then-current version of the services and [2] provide authorized users with enough instruction so that they can productively use the services. The documentation isn't necessarily a substitute for training, but the documentation must have the degree of specificity and ease of understanding such that it is instructive for the authorized users in their access and use of the services. A service provider may take issue with the characterization of "self-reliant" on the basis that there are different degrees of user sophistication and that the service provider's documentation doesn't cover the broad spectrum of sophistication.   Replacing that characterization with a lower threshold is a reasonable concession if you need to make a concession. For example, replacing "can become self-reliant with respect to access and use of the Services" with "can access and reasonably use the Services" may be, well, reasonable.

In the past, documentation was a revenue stream for some unscrupulous licensors, who charged licensees for making their own copies of documentation over some specified quantity.   That unsavory practice is mostly history now, but, just to be clear, language is included in this provision which allows you to [3] make as many copies of the documentation as required without additional charge (provided that the use of the documentation is for the sole purpose of using the services). Obviously, that assumes hardcopy documentation is even available.

While this provision is mostly innocuous, there's a component of it that could prove particularly beneficial to you and detrimental to the service provider. In the SaaS Agreement, the service provider represents and warrants that the services will conform in all material ways to the documentation (see the *Representations and Warranties – By Service Provider* provision). It's unlikely that a service provider will object to that commonplace and mostly insignificant representation and warranty. However, when "documentation" is robustly defined, the representation and warranty therefore becomes more substantial. Here, in the *Documentation* provision, the [1] documentation is defined as fully describing the then-current version of the services. Thus, when the robust definition of documentation is combined with the above representation and warranty, and the services subsequently don't conform to the documentation or vice versa, a service provider could be on the wrong end of a material breach.

As a side note, taking what could be objectionable contract language and then parsing it into smaller pieces of seemingly innocuous or less objectionable language across the length of a contract is a negotiation technique to watch for (or use). Pick the disparate pieces out of the contract and then read them together, and, oops, there's a problem for someone. This provision is an example of that technique. Documentation is defined in a robust manner, which, on its face, isn't objectionable. Much later in the SaaS Agreement and separated by a sea of words, documentation is used as a defined term in a representation and warranty that, similarly, isn't usually objectionable. Put together contractually, the combined language proves to be helpful to you and potentially detrimental to the service provider. If documentation was defined within the body of the representation and warranty or defined nearer to the representation and warranty, it would be more probable that a service provider would better link the two together and realize the risk (and object to it).

1.7   Documentation. The [1]documentation for the Services (the "Documentation") will accurately and completely describe the functions and features of the Services, including all subsequent revisions thereto.   The Documentation shall be [2]understandable by a typical end user and shall provide Authorized Users with sufficient instruction such that an Authorized User can become self-reliant with respect to access and use of the Services. Subscriber shall have the [3]right to make any number of additional copies of the Documentation at no additional charge.

Changes in Functionality

Another name for the *Changes in Functionality* provision could be the "bait and switch" provision. Some large software vendors (and SaaS service providers) have been known to eliminate or reduce functionality in one product or service and then introduce that same functionality (sometimes slightly enhanced as to disguise it) in a new product or service. Unwitting customers are duped into buying the "new" functionality and end up paying twice for it. Astute customers have caught on to the ploy and the "bait and switch" provision resulted. It's unfortunate that a provision like this exists, but there have been enough "bait and switch" instances that it's necessary.

[1] The service provider is prohibited from reducing or eliminating functionality in the services. It's uncommon for a service provider to object to this language, but an objection is a red flag and an indication that you're dealing with a service provider who either has pulled a bait and switch on its subscribers in the past or plans on doing so in the future. An objection should prompt you to probe the service provider. Has the service provider ever reduced or eliminated functionality in the past? If so, how were subscribers impacted? If not, are there plans to do so in the future? If there aren't any plans, then why is the language objectionable? [2] Where the service provider breaches the prohibition, you have the right to [3] terminate the services, be refunded any prepaid fees (not just for the services, but any other fees such as storage fees), and still be entitled to other damages. Terminating is a relatively unattractive remedy

with this breach and a service provider knows that, so it probably won't be too concerned with the remedy of termination. A service provider would bet you won't terminate because you need the remaining services and, therefore, you are more apt to pay the additional fees for the lost functionality in the "new" services. You do, however, have the right to seek damages for the breach if you're willing to go that route. As an alternative, and better, remedy, [4] you can determine, in your own opinion, the value of the reduced or eliminated functionality and the service provider is required to reduce the future services fees in an amount consistent with the value you determine. Because of the subjective nature of this language (i.e., you get to decide), a service provider is likely to object strenuously to this language. That objection is an invitation for you to craft a more objective method to determine the lost value. Further, [5] if the service provider ends up including the same or similar functionality in other services, you have the license to use those other services at no charge. This remedy doesn't quite make sense with [3] the first remedy since the originally contracted-for services will be terminated by you, but it's possible that you only have a need for the lost functionality and a license to the "new" services is sufficient. A license to the "new" services is likely to be objectionable in light of [4] the second remedy because you still have access to full functionality (albeit as a combined result of the originally contracted-for services and, now, in "new" separate services) and you now get to pay a lower price for that same full functionality. The counter-objection is that the service provider didn't have the right to eliminate or reduce the services to begin with and that you're now inconvenienced because, to obtain the full functionality, there are two separate services you have to use (whereas there was previously only one).

Going a bit further than language that's typically found in this type of bait and switch provision, [6] you have the right to any new functionality that the service provider introduces into the services. A service provider may balk at this right if new releases or versions are only available for an additional fee. Typically, however, with SaaS, new functionality in the form of enhancements that are introduced into the services is almost always included in the services fee. However, if that's not the case with your service provider and that wasn't entirely clear to you, it will certainly become obvious should the service provider make an objection.

1.8   <u>Changes in Functionality</u>. During the term of an <u>Exhibit A</u>, [1]Service Provider shall not reduce or eliminate functionality in the Services. [2]Where Service Provider has reduced or eliminated functionality in the Services, Subscriber, at Subscriber's sole election and in Subscriber's sole determination, shall: [3](a) have, in addition to any other rights and remedies under this Agreement or at law, the right to immediately terminate this Agreement or the <u>Exhibit A</u> and be entitled to a return of any prepaid fees; or, [4](b) determine the value of the reduced or eliminated functionality and Service Provider will immediately adjust the Services Fees accordingly on a prospective basis. [5]Where Service Provider has introduced like functionality in other services, Subscriber shall have an additional license and subscription right to use and access the new services, at no additional charge, with the same rights, obligations, and limitations as for the Services. [6]Where Service Provider increases functionality in the Services, such functionality shall be provided to Subscriber without any increase in the Services Fees.

No Effect of Click-Through Terms and Conditions

So-called click-through license agreements—where a user accesses software and is then presented with an on-screen agreement that he or she must accept (or not)—are sometimes used in SaaS, even SaaS where a subscriber already entered into a written agreement. In that case, there is the real dilemma that the click-through agreement amends the written agreement or takes precedence and supersedes the written agreement entirely. This dilemma is commonly referred to as the "battle of the forms," which is further explained under the *Non-Binding Terms* provision contained later in the SaaS Agreement.

Since you and the service provider are entering into the SaaS Agreement, it's obvious that the intent is for that agreement to govern and not a click-through agreement, so the service provider shouldn't have any real objection to the language of this provision. The only possible objections are that the provision isn't necessary because of the *Entire Agreement* provision or that the service provider doesn't have any click-through terms and conditions and the provision is therefore unnecessary. To the first objection, your argument should be that the *No Effect of Click-Through Terms and Conditions* provision just makes the *Entire Agreement* provision clearer. To the second objection, you should still insist on the provision being included as the service provider could add click-through terms and conditions in the future. Another reason for insisting on the provision's inclusion is that the language goes beyond invalidating a click-through agreement—it also [1] invalidates any terms and conditions, including terms of use, that a user isn't required to accept or reject but is instead made subject to as a result of the user's mere use of the services.

1.9   <u>No Effect of Click-Through Terms and Conditions</u>. Where an Authorized User is required to "click through" or otherwise accept or [1]made subject to any online terms and conditions in accessing or using the Services, such terms and conditions are not binding and shall have no force or effect as to the Services, this Agreement, or the applicable <u>Exhibit A</u>.

Service Levels

To measure service provider performance and as a means to mitigate performance risk, subscribers commonly employ the use of service levels. A service level is a tangible performance metric that defines a subscriber's service expectation and provides a performance standard for the service provider. A service level typically includes the payment of liquidated damages by the service provider for not achieving some pre-determined service level threshold. More bluntly, a service level is a widely used "get what you pay for" tool, and, if you don't get what you pay for, a service level is an easy way to be compensated for substandard performance. Note that liquidated damages for missed service levels are sometimes incorrectly referred to as "penalties." Penalties are generally not permitted under contract law because it's the job of the courts, and not private citizens, to penalize or punish. Less frequently—and *not* the case with the SaaS Agreement—a service level includes the payment of rewards (as an incentive) by a subscriber when the service provider exceeds service levels.

There are two primary reasons why subscribers request service level liquidated damages: to recover business costs (such as the fee paid for the SaaS) associated with a missed service level; or, to induce the service provider to achieve service levels through negative reinforcement in the form of liquidated damages. There is some debate as to whether liquidated damages prompt desired performance. Such damages may even have a negative effect on a subscriber in terms of service provider pricing: even where service providers are generally capable of achieving a service level, service providers commonly increase prices to mitigate any possible future liquidated damages paid out due to missed service levels.

An alternative model that is not contemplated by the SaaS Agreement but is worthy of some discussion here are service levels with service provider-oriented escalations instead of liquidated damages. Escalation paths, unlike liquidated damages as a mere financial transaction, tend to ensure visibility of service provider non-performance to increasing levels of subscriber and service provider management. Under this alternative model, each management level of a service provider must answer to the next level of the service provider's management *and* the subscriber's management where the service provider did not achieve a service level. The effects on a service provider's human and organizational behavior in this type of service level model can have a significant and far-reaching impact, with resulting tangible benefits for the subscriber. The escalation model also forces "partnership-in-practice" behavior. As much as subscribers hope to believe that their service providers are business partners, a service provider is, and will always be, a service provider.

Service levels with liquidated damages tend to be contractually oriented buyer-seller procurement relationships, where the impact of an unachieved service level is in the form of a quantitative, financial transaction. Consequently, the liquidated damages model does little to bring a subscriber and service provider closer together in terms of the business relationship. In contrast, service levels with organizational peer-to-peer escalations tend to drive deeper relationships, with the service provider being more inclined to understand the adverse business implications to the subscriber of unachieved service levels. The primary objective of the service level with escalations model is to ensure the service provider keenly understands that its relationship with the subscriber centers on achieving required service levels. Should you wish to replace the traditional liquidated damages service level model that is used in the SaaS Agreement, or augment that model by incorporating elements of the escalation model, here are some items that the escalation model or a hybrid model focus on and encompass: (a) detailed peer-to-peer escalation procedures, to include escalation "triggers" and timeframes for escalation to the next level where resolution is not achieved; (b) predetermined set of actions to occur when performance measurement points are below minimum service level targets (the escalation trigger); (c) clear identification of escalation levels (peers, by name and title), responsibilities, and accountability; (d) methodology for a joint problem resolution process; (e) post-mortem procedures defined for root cause analyses; (f) goals for long-term improvement, both process and relationship; (g) agreement to act on the intent of the contract, rather than solely on the written content; and, (h) an operating principle of fairness, not exploitation of any contract inefficiencies.

As earlier indicated, the SaaS Agreement includes the traditional service levels with liquidated damages model. The *Service Levels* section sets forth that model in a very straight-forward manner: the section refers to Exhibit A where the service levels are described (see the *Exhibit A – Services Levels* section for the actual descriptions); service level reporting requirements are described; the consequences of failure are described; and the subscriber's right to audit the service provider is established.

Be prepared for some contentious discussions with a service provider regarding the various provisions contained in this *Service Levels* section. No service provider enjoys having its feet held to the fire in terms of performing, particularly when it involves liquidated damages and possible contract termination resulting from the service provider's substandard performance. However, more mature and capable service providers are used to service levels and even offer them (albeit somewhat toothless) in their own SaaS contract templates. You'll get a sense of how mature and / or capable your service provider is based on the degree to which it takes issue with this section. Whether the complaining from your service provider is significant or not, know that this section and the service levels described in Exhibit A are mostly fair and balanced. This section of the SaaS Agreement strives to ensure that you get what you pay for, and, if not, you have recourse and will be made whole. Despite what a service provider might want to convince you to believe, you need some mechanism to hold a service provider accountable for performing—and that's the reason for this section and service levels. Without service levels and some sort of corresponding remedies, good luck when your service provider doesn't perform.

Service Levels; Time is of the Essence

Since service levels may be different based on the services being provided, may be adjusted over time, or may be added after contracting, the details of service levels are better suited for an Exhibit A (which describes, in detail, the scope of the services being performed). In this *Service Levels; Time is of the Essence* provision, the connection between the performance of the services and the service levels is made, subject to a force majeure event (see the *Force Majeure; Excused Performance* provision for a description of what constitutes a force majeure event). To emphasize the importance of timeliness of performance, [1] "time is of the essence" language is included. When "time is of the essence" isn't expressly included in a contract, courts generally permit a party to perform its obligations within a reasonable time (whatever that means). When "time is of the essence" is included, the failure of a party to perform within the time required constitutes a material breach of the contract. With SaaS, particularly as it relates to availability of the services, time is clearly important. Unfortunately, even first-year law students recognize that "time is of the essence" lays a substantial burden and risk on the party with the obligation to perform. If that party is late in performing—even minutely late—it's a material breach and gives the non-breaching party tremendous leverage (up to and including contract termination). Thus, it's highly likely a service provider will balk at the "time is of the essence" language. Your counter-argument is that the availability of the services is critically important to you but that there is some leeway since the obligation of paying liquidated damages for the availability service level is set to begin at some level less than 100% availability; therefore, the "time is of the essence" language should remain.

2.1   <u>Service Levels; [1]Time is of the Essence</u>. For the term of an <u>Exhibit A</u>, Service Provider shall provide the Services, force majeure events excepted, during the applicable Service Windows and in accordance with the applicable Service Level Standards, each as described in the <u>Exhibit A</u>, [1]time being of the essence.

The discussion of "time is of the essence" leads to a tangential, but important, point about one of the advantages of using your SaaS Agreement and not the service provider's contract template. Take a look at the provision following this paragraph—most contract templates have this provision, called a "headings" or "no headings" provision. As you can see in the following *Headings* provision, the language of the provision invalidates any contractual force of any heading in the contract. In short, the provision knocks headings down to something that's merely for the convenience of the parties. Almost every contract professional knows that almost every contract in the universe has a similar "headings" provision. In contrast, the SaaS Agreement *does not* have such a provision. The service provider's representative reviewing your SaaS Agreement will likely only glance at the headings because that person assumes, wrongly, you have a *Headings* provision like every other contract that person has ever seen. Instead, that person will concentrate on the body of the provisions: headings just don't get that much attention.

21.8.   Headings. Provision headings are for convenience or reference only and shall not be used to construe the meaning of any provision in this Agreement.

Now go back to the *Service Levels; Time is of the Essence* provision—it contains "time being of the essence" in the very last sentence. As previously indicated, the service provider is going to balk when it sees that language in the body of the provision and it's going to redline that language out. You're going to interrogate the service provider as to why it can't agree to that, why it can't commit to performing the services in a timely manner, that the service provider had said it was the best service provider in the world during the competitive bidding process, and so on. Unless you have a ton of leverage, you'll likely have to give up on the "time being of the essence" language—but you might be able to trade it for some other concession. As a result, the service provider, in a hurry, is going to be pleased it got the language out and will move on to the next provision.

Well, remember the heading, the underlined part of the *Service Levels; Time is of the Essence* provision? The part that states *Time is of the Essence?* What contract professionals frequently miss is redlining the "time is of the essence" language from the provision's heading. They're so used to seeing a *Headings* provision near the end of contracts in the miscellaneous boilerplate section that they're asleep at the wheel when it comes to headings. Because there's no *Headings* provision in the SaaS Agreement that invalidates the language contained in a header, you get your "time is of the essence" language with all its power.

The moral of this tangential topic is that a service provider's contract template is going to be loaded with similar "gotchas."

You're better off not trying to comb through the service provider's contract template to find and defuse the land mines; instead, use your own tried-and-true SaaS Agreement.

Service Level Reporting

To monitor a service provider's performance as compared to service levels, detailed reporting provided to you on a regular basis is an absolute necessity. Under the SaaS Agreement, the [1] service provider must provide you with reports on the 15th of every month during the term which describes services performance against the service level standards (for each one of the service levels) for the prior month. The implication of monthly reporting is that the services are measured for the purposes of service levels on a monthly basis. The tendency of service providers is to measure service against service level standards over a longer period of time, such as a quarter, so as to smooth out (via averaging) instances of subpar performance. Expect similar push back from your service provider. There is an exception [2] to that monthly reporting requirement for the subscriber satisfaction survey, which is conducted and measured on an annual "contract year" basis.

The form of the reporting [3] is something that you must agree to. While you don't have the right to specify the form of the report (obviously, you can change the language of the provision if you do want that right), there are some basic elements that are required to be included in a service level report: (a) what the performance was and how that compares to what the performance should have been; (b) why the performance was subpar if it was subpar; (c) what the service provider is going to do in the future in the case of subpar performance to ensure it doesn't occur again; and, (d) what liquidated damages (in the form of a performance credit), if any, are due. A service provider may get fussy about having to explain what it's going to do to make sure a service level problem doesn't occur again as that process of explaining means having to do root causes analyses and then developing remedial measures (read: work the service provider doesn't want to do). Considering that, if a service provider starts chipping away at the list of what needs to be included in a service level report, be prepared to stand firm with the position that the list represents the most basic reporting elements—and that anything less will dilute the purpose of having service levels to begin with.

To ensure that you and the service provider have a disciplined process for monitoring performance on an ongoing basis, the [4] service provider is required to meet with you monthly—or as often as you reasonably request it (but don't abuse the privilege). Based on the size of your account, a service provider may want to tweak the language to ensure that telephone or online meetings, rather than only face-to-face, are permissible. You'll have to determine what makes sense for you, but, if you're a large account for the service provider, a face-to-face meeting format is likely the best way to ensure the right level of attention from the service provider. It's also the best format for working through any performance issues.

Sometimes a service provider fails to provide service level reporting in a timely manner. There might be a variety of reasons for that, none of which is probably a valid or acceptable reason for you. It's also not helpful when, anecdotally or experientially, you *know* that service levels have been missed but you're not getting the reports to validate performance (and you're not getting the liquidated damages that you believe are owed to you). Further, it's a waste of your time to have to chase down the service provider to provide the reporting. To avoid all of the foregoing, and to act as a deterrent for late reporting, [5] any service level for which you're not provided a report when due is considered completely failed. That means you'll get any corresponding liquidated damages. A service provider isn't going to like this language and will probably strike it. This is your opportunity to question the service provider as to why it can't provide timely reports—again, the service provider isn't likely to have a valid or acceptable reason. Rather than strike the language, a service provider may offer a compromise: for example, instead of "completely failed," setting a different threshold that will result in liquidated damages less than what they would have been at the "completely failed" level. Be leery of any compromises with this language and think about possible unintended consequences. While the foregoing compromise sounds reasonable, it could result in a service provider actually completely failing a service level, intentionally not providing a report for that service level, and then only having to pay liquidated damages equivalent to some level other than the actual completely failed level.

Over time, it's easy to misfile or misplace service level reports, so it makes sense to go back to the originator of the reports, the service provider, to get old reports. Unfortunately, this has happened often enough that service providers started charging for historical reports as a deterrent. Of course, under the SaaS Agreement, [6] old reports are to be provided without charge and that might be objectionable to the service provider. A reasonable alternative is for the service provider to provide you with access to a portal where the historical service level reports are archived.

2.2   Service Level Reporting. [1]On a monthly basis, in arrears and no later than the fifteenth (15th) calendar day of the subsequent month following the reporting month, Service Provider shall provide reports to Subscriber describing the performance of the Services and of Service Provider as compared to the Service Level Standards; provided, however, that [2]the Subscriber Satisfaction Survey Service Level shall be conducted by Service Provider each year on the anniversary of the Effective Date and the results shall be reported to Subscriber by Service Provider no later than the fifteenth (15th) calendar day of the subsequent month following such anniversary date. [3]The reports shall be in a form agreed-to by Subscriber, and, in no case, contain no less than the following information: (a) actual performance compared to the Service Level Standard; (b) the cause or basis for not meeting the Service Level Standard; (c) the specific remedial actions Service Provider has undertaken or will undertake to ensure that the Service Level Standard will be subsequently achieved; and, (d) any Performance Credit due to Subscriber. Service Provider and Subscriber [4]will meet as often as shall be reasonably requested by Subscriber, but no less than monthly, to review the performance of Service Provider as it relates to the Service Levels. [5]Where Service Provider fails to provide a report for a Service Level in the applicable timeframe, the Service Level shall be deemed to be completely failed for the purposes of calculating a Performance Credit.

[6]Service Provider shall, without charge, make Subscriber's historical Service Level reports to Subscriber upon request.

Failure to Meet Service Level Standards

In the SaaS Agreement, the service level standards are pegged at optimal performance. For example, the service level standard for the availability service level that is contained in the sample Exhibit A is 100%. That standard might seem, particularly to a service provider, a lofty and perhaps unattainable goal. It's no goal; rather, it's an expectation. You certainly didn't intend to contract and pay for something less than 100% performance. So why should your service level standards reflect anything less than 100% performance? A service provider will argue that it can't guarantee 100% performance 100% of the time. On that basis, your service level standards should be pegged at something less than 100%. While that sounds like a rational argument on its face, it's not in the context of the SaaS Agreement and the service levels described in Exhibit A. First, certain service levels have contingencies already built into them. Using the availability service level as an example, scheduled downtime for such things as maintenance doesn't count against the availability service level standard. It's when the services are scheduled to be available but aren't available that the service level standard of 100% is dinged. Second, none of the service levels requires a payout in the form of performance credits as liquidated damages when the service provider misses the 100% service level standard. In the case of availability, a performance credit doesn't kick in until availability is equal to or less than 99.98%. While a .02% difference might seem negligible, when you consider the tens of thousands of minutes in a month as well as excused downtime that doesn't get counted against the service provider (e.g., for maintenance), 99.98% starts looking pretty favorable for a service provider. In short, you're paying for 100% performance but no service provider is perfect, so, the service provider gets a pass on 100% performance up to a certain point. When the service provider hits that certain point or falls below it, it's required to refund you the difference (in the form of a performance credit as liquidated damages) of what you paid for and how the service provider ultimately performed. That's absolutely and perfectly reasonable. So when a service provider argues that it can't perform at 100% and your service level standard is unattainable, carefully explain that: (a) you expect 100% performance (because that's what you're paying for); (b) in some cases, there are built-in contingencies that favor the service provider; and, (c) that liquidated damages don't automatically kick-in if the service provider doesn't perform at 100%. To be confident in your explanation, you must thoroughly understand how the service levels described in Exhibit A work and that level of thoroughness can only be achieved by running example scenarios through a service level calculation. That might seem to be a lot of work, but investing in well-developed and unambiguous service levels translates into less arguing, angst, and time in the future regarding a service provider's subpar performance. It might take you more than one discussion to explain the service level standards to a service provider as the service provider might have a difficult time trying to wrap its collective mind around the concept that you want it to hit 100% but that the service provider doesn't necessarily have to pay up if it misses 100%. A service provider's lack of understanding isn't a valid reason to adjust a service level standard to something less than 100%.

The *Failure to Meet Service Level Standards* provision starts by specifying a **[1]** two-prong remedy for subpar performance. First, the **[2]** service provider shall "owe" to you "any applicable" performance credit. The "any applicable" language goes to a performance credit not being due until performance drops to the specified service level trigger point for liquidated damages, i.e., a performance credit isn't applicable until the service level calculation indicates that one is. "Owe" is used in the context of performance credits in combination with the *Credits* provision of the *Fees; Billing* section, which allows for the flexibility of applying performance credits against any amounts due to the service provider or, alternatively, obtaining any performance credits as a payment from the service provider. The contractual ability to apply performance credits against amounts due to a service provider is particularly helpful if, for whatever reason, the service provider fails to pay a performance credit (which happens with surprising frequency) that you believe you are due. In other words, if you are owed a performance credit and haven't received it, you can simply short pay the next service provider invoice.

While performance credits as compensation for a service provider's subpar performance is nice, that's not why you contracted with the service provider: you contracted to productively use the SaaS. That's where the second prong of the remedy comes into play. Not only is a performance credit due for subpar performance, the [3] service provider must use its "best efforts" to ensure that it doesn't blow the service level in the future. Service providers tend to get excited about anything that requires "best efforts." Many, including attorneys for service providers, wrongly believe that best efforts means an obligation to do everything in one's power, just short of bankrupting oneself in the process, to fulfill an obligation. However, while admittedly an amorphous term that is better replaced with words of specificity if possible, a best efforts standard isn't as onerous as most believe. Essentially, according to most courts, best efforts means to undertake all reasonable efforts and diligence to fulfill the corresponding obligation. If you can't convince a service provider that it should use its best (i.e., reasonable) efforts, then ask the service provider to be specific about what it *will* do to ensure future performance. If the service provider can commit to something that has specificity and substance, such as following a root cause analysis procedure, developing remedial actions, involving executives, and providing you with a detailed report of the analysis and corrective actions, then that might be something worthy of replacing the "best efforts" language. However, merely replacing "best efforts" with something weaker or more diluted (e.g., "commercially reasonable") clearly isn't helpful or favorable for you.

While the [1] two-prong remedy might help to make you whole after-the-fact, it doesn't do anything for you while you're in the midst of experiencing subpar performance. Thus, [4] when the service provider is faced with a situation that might or does result in subpar performance, the service provider must use best efforts to minimize the impact to you. Just as with [1] the two-prong remedy, the service provider may take issue with "best efforts." If the service provider has an alternative that is satisfactory to you and it's something better than "commercially reasonable," then the alternative is probably worth considering.

The provision wraps up [5] with an administrative item that addresses something occasionally found in service provider contract templates: the requirement to notify the service provider that you're due a performance credit within a specified period, and, if you don't provide such notice, you forfeit the performance credit. That's wholly unreasonable as the service provider is in a better position than you are to determine that a service level has been missed to the extent a performance credit is due. It's really a service provider ruse, hoping you forget to ask so that the service provider is off the hook for not performing and for not paying. Just to be clear, you are owed a performance credit when due whether you notified the service provider or not.

2.3   Failure to Meet Service Level Standards. As further described in an Exhibit A, [1]in the event Service Provider does not meet a Service Level Standard, Service Provider shall: [2](a) owe to Subscriber any applicable Performance Credit, as liquidated damages and not as a penalty; and, [3](b) use its best efforts to ensure that any unmet Service Level Standard is subsequently met. Notwithstanding the foregoing, [4]Service Provider will use its best efforts to minimize the impact or duration of any outage, interruption, or degradation of Service. [5]In no case shall Subscriber be required to notify Service Provider that a Performance Credit is due as a condition of payment of the same.

Termination for Material and Repeated Failures

The *Termination for Material and Repeated Failures* provision will likely be the most contentious of the *Service Levels* section. This provision gives you the [2] right to terminate the SaaS Agreement (or a specific Exhibit A in case there are other services under other exhibits that you don't want to terminate) where [4] the service provider's performance is so subpar that it materially disrupts your productive use of the services or because [5] the service provider has repeatedly missed service levels. Further, [1] that right isn't limited or exclusive—you still have the right to sue the service provider for damages as a result of the service provider's material breach of the SaaS Agreement. The reason that this provision is so contentious is because termination of the SaaS Agreement means [3] lost revenue that the service provider had been banking on. Losing what in some cases might be years of expected future revenue is a lot more painful for a service provider than having to pay liquidated damages every now and then for missed service levels.

[4] A service provider will almost certainly want to completely remove, or at the very least, chip away at your right to determine, in your opinion, whether the services were so subpar that your ability to use them was "materially disrupted." From a service provider's perspective, the right of termination represents too much subjectivity and too much leverage (for you). [5] If you can't argue to keep the language in, an acceptable fallback position is the right to terminate when the service provider repeatedly misses services levels—that acceptable fallback assumes the service provider doesn't dilute what triggers your remedy of termination. For example, a service provider may want to restrict the trigger to be based on *consecutive* months of its chronic failure to meet service levels or by restricting the measurement period. Here's an example using replacement language that restricts both the trigger and the timeframe: "(b) for three (3) consecutive months out of a contract year." That replacement language means the service provider can miserably fail a service level throughout most of a contract year and, as long as the service provider doesn't fail it for 3-months in a row, you don't have a right to terminate. That also means the service provider can fail to hit a service level for the last 2-months of a contract year and fail the first 2-months of the next contract year without triggering your right to terminate. That's 4-months of consecutively failed service levels and you still won't have a right to terminate. The existing language—a specified number of months within a specified period—is very fair.

If you have to cave on **[4]** your right to terminate in the case of material disruption for repeated failures but you get some other unrelated concession in return, that might be a reasonable trade. However, you'll need to stand your ground with the service provider on **[5]** the trigger and timeframe for repeated failures.

2.3.1   <u>Termination for Material and Repeated Failures</u>.   Subscriber shall have, [1]in addition to any other rights and remedies under this Agreement or at law, the [2]right to immediately terminate this Agreement or an <u>Exhibit A,</u> and be entitled to a [3]return of any prepaid fees where Service Provider fails to meet any Service Level Standard: [4](a) to such an extent that the Subscriber's ability, as solely determined by Subscriber, to use the Services is materially disrupted, force majeure events excepted; or, [5](b) for four (4) months out of any twelve (12) month period.

Audit of Service Levels

To assure yourself that service levels have been calculated correctly by a service provider, it's necessary to audit the service provider's records. The *Audit of Service Levels* provision **[1]** preserves your right of audit for both service level *and* performance credit calculations. However, as you don't want the service provider to audit your use of the services, a service provider isn't going to want to be subjected to an audit related to service levels. Be prepared for a service provider to do a wholesale strike of this provision; however, you should be able to convince a service provider to allow you to conduct some sort of reasonable audit (particularly if the service provider demands its right to audit you) or to at least provide you with supporting detail on request. **[2]** While service levels are reported on a monthly basis (excluding the subscriber satisfaction survey service level), the provision restricts your audits to a quarterly frequency. Any more than that will likely be administratively burdensome or expensive and a service provider isn't going to be happy—because of the invasive nature of any audit—to do it any more frequently. It's very likely that a service provider will modify the language to limit the frequency to no more than annually. Since you may not have the staff or skillsets necessary to conduct a thorough audit, [3] you have the option of hiring a third-party to serve as your agent in conducting an audit. A service provider doesn't like an experienced third-party auditor rifling through its records because there's a greater likelihood the auditor will uncover an error than you. Don't be surprised if a service provider takes issue with that language. [4] If it turns out that the service provider did make an error, you are owed the correct performance credit, if any. Similar to the *Failure to Meet Service Level Standards* provision, "owe" (rather than, for example, "shall be paid") is used in the context of performance credits in combination with the *Credits* provision of the *Fees; Billing* section, which allows you to apply the performance credits against any amounts due to the service provider or, alternatively, obtaining the performance credits as a payment from the service provider.

2.4   <u>Audit of Service Levels</u>. [2]No more than quarterly, Subscriber or [3]Subscriber's agent shall have the [1]right to audit Service Provider's books, records, and measurement and auditing tools to verify Service Level Standard achievement and to determine correct payment of any Performance Credit. [4]Where it is determined that any Performance Credit was due to Subscriber but not paid, Service Provider shall immediately owe to Subscriber the applicable Performance Credit.

Support; Maintenance; Additional Services

Other than the *Maintenance* provision, the provisions within this section are simple and merely link the master agreement component (the "legal" terms) of the SaaS Agreement to the exhibit component (the "business" terms contained in an Exhibit A). Each of the provisions assumes that there are no additional fees for the described ancillary services and that the services fees are "all-in" and inclusive of the ancillary services. Your service provider may routinely charge for such ancillary services, but all-in services fees should be your starting point for negotiations. If you include the SaaS Agreement as a part of your competitive bid so that bidders can review your contract template, you're telegraphing to the bidders that you expect all-in services fees—if a bidder has an issue with that, the bidder can take exception as a part of the proposal. If you end up agreeing to a separate fee for one or more ancillary services, you can include the fee within the applicable section on the Exhibit A.

Technical Support

The description and detail of technical support are described in the *Exhibit A – Technical Support Description* and *Exhibit A – Technical Support Problem Severity Levels* sections. If your requirements for technical support are different, which is likely, you'll need to modify Exhibit A accordingly. If you are unable to negotiate all-in services fees, be aware that fees for technical support (which sometimes includes maintenance) can range from 5% to 20% of the annualized subscription fee. Be sure to include caps on fees for technical support so that the fees either are capped for the duration of the Exhibit A or are limited in the amount of increases.

3.1   Technical Support. Service Provider shall provide the Technical Support described in an Exhibit A. The Services Fees shall be inclusive of the fees for the Technical Support.

Maintenance

Maintenance typically includes [1] bug fixes, corrections, and other modifications necessary to ensure that the services function in accordance with the corresponding documentation. [2] For those maintenance services that are necessary to ensure the SaaS works as advertised, it's inappropriate to be charged an additional fee. You've already paid for the SaaS and how it's expected to perform, so, when it doesn't perform as expected, why should you have to pay for the service provider to fix it and bring it up to the correct specifications? Well, you shouldn't, and if the service provider requests a fee for maintenance, ask questions and probe why that isn't already built into the services fees and why you should pay for the service provider to correct deficiencies that are its fault.

While the service provider responsibilities detailed in the *Maintenance* provision are very typical for this type of provision, **[3]** there's additional language in this provision that goes a bit further and that you may have to agree to strike as a trade for not being charged for maintenance. In addition to the typical bug fixes, corrections, and modifications to ensure conformance to the documentation, a service provider is also required by this provision to provide enhancements, upgrades, and new releases—all at no additional charge. A service provider may immediately object to this and point out that such increases in functionality would be an additional charge.

The more standard language in this provision requires the service provider to **[4]** maintain the services such that the services function in accordance with the documentation and requires that **[5]** the maintenance services comport with the applicable portions of the *Representations and Warranties* section; specifically to *not* introduce a mechanism to disable any part of the services (which could be used by the service provider to hold you hostage if you don't pay timely and so on—keep in mind, though, a service provider could just "flip the switch" and kill the services) and to ensure the services conform in all material respects to the specifications, functions, descriptions, standards, and criteria in the Exhibit A and the documentation. The service provider is **[6]** also obligated to do necessary work (i.e., provide maintenance) on the services to ensure that the service levels can be met. Finally, **[7]** considering that some organizations don't always implement the latest and greatest technology (and for good reason), the service provider must maintain the capability of the services to function with prior versions of popular web browsers (if you use a different browser or something proprietary, you should add that browser to this list).

Similar to the *Technical Support* provision, if you are unable to negotiate all-in services fees, be aware that fees for maintenance can also range from 5% to 20% of the annualized subscription fee. According to industry research at the time of this book's publication, if you're being charged a separate fee for technical support and another separate fee for maintenance and, combined, the fees exceed 30%, it's very likely that the service provider is bilking you. Be sure to include caps on fees for maintenance so that the fees either are capped for the duration of the Exhibit A or are limited in the amount of increases.

3.2   <u>Maintenance</u>. Service Provider shall provide [1]bug fixes, corrections, modifications, [3]enhancements, upgrades, and new releases to the Services to ensure: [4](a) the functionality of the Services, as described in the Documentation, is available to Authorized Users; [5](b) the functionality of the Services in accordance with the representations and warranties set forth herein, including but not limited to, the Services conforming in all material respects to the specifications, functions, descriptions, standards, and criteria set forth in the applicable <u>Exhibit A</u>; [6](c) the Service Level Standards can be achieved; and, [7](d) the Services work with the then-current version and the three prior versions of Internet Explorer, Mozilla Firefox, and Google Chrome Internet browsers. [2]The Services Fees shall be inclusive of the fees for maintenance.

Required Notice of Maintenance

Subscribers are sometimes surprised when a service provider introduces what some call "silent" or "stealth" maintenance. The surprise is usually an unpleasant one for a subscriber and is most obvious when the services interface changes or some other user-oriented functionality changes. Even worse are the "surprises" that initially go unnoticed such as changes to data edits or data formats. Once maintenance is elevated to production, a service provider is loath to back it out. To avoid such problems, you need to be aware of impending changes, what the changes include, when the changes will occur, and what the impact is, if any, to you. With that said, there are circumstances in which maintenance is needed to address emergency situations to, for example, avoid services downtime or data integrity problems.

The *Required Notice of Maintenance* provision attempts to balance the need for you to be notified of, and to adequately prepare for, maintenance with the possible need of the service provider to perform maintenance in an emergency. [1] Unless you otherwise agree, the service provider must, as a default, provide 30-days advance notice of non-emergency maintenance. Some service providers won't like the length of the period, and if your service provider expresses concern, it's a possible indication that it doesn't do a very good job of planning and scheduling maintenance. Remind the service provider that the 30-calendar day period is only a default and a shorter notice period can be accommodated on an as-needed basis. So you know what to test (or what internal business processes, documentation, and so on that you'll need to adjust), the service provider must [2] provide you with a description of the maintenance being elevated to production.

While maintenance should be something that can be planned for in a methodical and scheduled way, even the best of service providers will occasionally have a need to introduce emergency maintenance. In those cases, the service provider is obligated to [3] provide you as much advance notice as possible, but, ultimately, doesn't need to provide you with any notice. Since, by its very nature, an emergency is difficult to define, the term "emergency" as used in this provision is not defined and is therefore ambiguous. Thus, you need to be wary of a service provider that begins to have more and more frequent so-called "emergency" maintenance—that's a sign that the emergency maintenance isn't really an emergency and that the service provider has figured out a way around providing you the required notice for non-emergency maintenance. Following the elevation of the emergency maintenance to production and [4] within 1-calendar day, the service provider is required to provide you with a description of the maintenance. As a negotiation concession, you may have to increase the period, but anything beyond 3-business days is too long.

3.2.1 <u>Required Notice of Maintenance</u>. [1]Unless as otherwise agreed to by Subscriber on a case-by-case basis, Service Provider shall provide no less than thirty (30) calendar day's prior written notice to Subscriber of all non-emergency maintenance to be performed on the Services, such written notice [2]including a detailed description of all maintenance to be performed. [3]For emergency maintenance, Service Provider shall provide as much prior notice as commercially practicable to Subscriber and shall provide a [4]detailed description of all maintenance performed no greater than one (1) calendar day following the implementation of the emergency maintenance.

Acceptance of Non-Emergency Maintenance

Once you've been given the required notice by the service provider for *non-emergency* maintenance, you have a [1] 10-business day period to test the proposed maintenance. That period may be too long in some cases and too short in others, thus [2] the default period of 10-business days can be adjusted, subject to your approval, on a case-by-case basis. To be consistent with commitments made to other subscribers, a service provider may request that the default period be set to something less than 10-business days and / or request that the default period be an absolute (i.e., a maximum period) that is not subject to increase. [3] If you have a valid reason to reject any proposed maintenance (for example, a maintenance change may fail to work properly as a result of your testing), you have the right to make such a rejection and the service provider is not permitted to elevate the rejected maintenance to production. [4] If you fail to complete testing within the applicable period or you fail to provide notice of any rejections—which is not the fault of the service provider—the service provider has the right to elevate the maintenance to production.

3.2.2 <u>Acceptance of Non-Emergency Maintenance</u>. Unless as otherwise agreed to by Subscriber on a [2]case-by-case basis, [1]for non-emergency maintenance, Subscriber shall have a ten (10) business day period to test any maintenance changes prior to Service Provider introducing such maintenance changes into production (the "Maintenance Acceptance

The Master Software as a Service Agreement

Period"). [3]In the event that Subscriber rejects, for good cause, any maintenance changes during the Maintenance Acceptance Period, Service Provider shall not introduce such rejected maintenance changes into production. [4]At the end of the Maintenance Acceptance Period, if Subscriber has not rejected the maintenance changes, the maintenance changes shall be deemed to be accepted by Subscriber and Service Provider shall be entitled to introduce the maintenance changes into production.

Customization / Integration Services

The actual description and detail of customization / integration services are described in the *Exhibit A – Customization / Integration Services* section. The customization / integration services would include anything you need to have performed to use the services in the manner desired by you. For example, customization / integration could be as simple as adding your company's logo on the SaaS portal to as complicated as building interfaces between your systems and the SaaS. If your situation leans toward the more complicated, you may want to consider a completely separate Exhibit A to describe all of the requirements, deliverables, project schedule, and so on. If you expect to use customization / integration services over the long term, you'll want to lock in, if possible, time and material rates or other rates so as to avoid future increases. These set rates or caps on rates should be described in the *Exhibit A – Customization / Integration Services* section. If you don't need any customization / integration services, this provision can remain in the SaaS Agreement because the language of the provision acknowledges via "if any" that such services may not be needed for a particular Exhibit A.

3.3   <u>Customization / Integration Services</u>.   Service Provider shall provide the Customization / Integration Services, if any, described in an <u>Exhibit A</u>. The Services Fees shall be inclusive of the fees for the Customization / Integration Services.

Training Services

The actual description and detail of training services are described in the *Exhibit A – Training Services* section. The training services would include anything authorized users would need to initially use the services and any sort of refresher training. Consider also that you'll likely add new authorized users over time that weren't in the first round of training, so you'll need some sort of training mechanism to get those authorized users trained on the services. Similar to customization / integration services, if you have more complex training requirements (such as customized training), you may want to consider a completely separate Exhibit A to describe all of the requirements, deliverables, project schedule, and so on. In any case, be sure to clearly specify the type of training and method of delivery such as web-based or computer-based, instructor-led, or train-the-trainer. Since it's likely you'll need training services in the future, you'll want to lock in, if possible, time and material rates or other rates so as to avoid future increases. These set rates or caps on rates should be described in the *Exhibit A – Training Services* section. If you don't need any training services, this provision can remain in the SaaS Agreement because the language of the provision acknowledges via "if any" that such services may not be needed for a particular Exhibit A.

3.4   <u>Training Services</u>. Service Provider shall provide the Training Services, if any, described in an <u>Exhibit A</u>. The Services Fees shall be inclusive of the fees for the Training Services.

Escrow Agreement

As explained in the *Introduction*, SaaS is a trade-off of sorts: you get ease-of-deployment and a lower capital investment but, at the same time, you lose control by not having the software installed on your technology infrastructure and your data residing on your premises. You also take on risks inherent to SaaS such as service interruptions and downtime. Those risks are in addition to those encountered with traditional software licensing, for example, bankruptcy, ceased operations, change of control, and failure to maintain. Under traditional software licensing, many of the potential risks are mitigated through escrow. In short, software escrow is the deposit by the licensor of the software (usually source code) with a third-party escrow agent, with the software released to the licensee when some default event occurs so that the licensee can continue to use the software. Escrow for SaaS (which is software) works essentially the same way. Ultimately, however, you really don't want the software: unless you've made arrangements with a third-party (discussed further below), you probably won't even know what to do with the software if and when you get it. The useful purpose of escrow is to serve as a deterrent for the licensor (or service provider in the case of SaaS). Licensors and service providers don't want their valuable intellectual property (in the form of software) "on the streets" if they can avoid it, so they do what they need in order to avoid triggering the release of their software from escrow.

As a part of its escrow obligations, the service provider is required to [1] place in escrow—at no cost to you—the most recent version of the source and object code that is used to provide the services along with all of the components and documentation necessary for you to run and use the software on your own technology infrastructure. Should anything occur that demonstrates, in your sole determination, the service provider is [2] unable or unwilling to provide the Services, you have [3] the right to obtain the software from the escrow agent. There are two schools of thought when it comes to software escrow. One school of thought is that a software license or SaaS contract requires, as an exhibit, a comprehensive three-way escrow agreement ratified by the licensor / service provider, licensee / subscriber, and escrow agent. The other, less-widely adopted, school of thought is to include a simple few-sentence paragraph in the body of the contract between the licensor / service provider and licensee / subscriber.

A comprehensive escrow agreement contains "triggers" (typically called "events of default" or "default events") that, when they occur, require the escrow agent to deliver the software to the licensee / subscriber. This type of escrow agreement also contains all sorts of formalities as it relates to notice of default and so on. Here's the basic, fundamental problem: the more precise the default events in their description, the more likely the event that actually occurs doesn't trigger escrow. In other words, what happens if one of the default events described in the escrow agreement doesn't occur but some other event that you haven't foreseen does occur and impacts the service provider's ability to provide the services? Oops, too bad for you, because it's not described in the escrow agreement as a default event. Also, generally, the escrow agent must agree that the default event has occurred. Sure, they're supposed to be neutral and independent, but do you think escrow agents really are? Do you think they'd be in business for long if they had a reputation of giving up software without putting up a fuss first? Also, you have to keep an eye on the procedures for notice. One slip up on your part and you may not be entitled to the software.

In comparison, the other school of thought—the few sentences of escrow language in the body of the contract—is very broad but clear: if the service provider demonstrates an [2] "inability or unwillingness" to fulfill any of its obligations under the SaaS Agreement, you get a copy of the software—period. The escrow agent can't balk and nit-pick over whether a default event occurred not only because of the use of plain language but also because the escrow agent isn't a party to the SaaS Agreement. You could care less what the agreement between the escrow agent and the service provider says. You don't have to worry about complicated notice procedures or wait through a notice period. You can march down to the courthouse and get specific performance if the escrow agent doesn't comply by releasing the software. When it comes to contract language, sometimes "less is more" and this is a perfect example.

Even if you go the route of "less is more," service providers sometimes want to include their agreement with the escrow agent as an exhibit to the SaaS Agreement. You should avoid that. Even though you're not a party to the agreement between the service provider and escrow agent, merely including it as an exhibit to your SaaS Agreement could mean that you've acquiesced to its terms (and default events).

As a means to verify that the service provider is performing its escrow obligations, you have two options. You can decide to [4] use your own agent (at your cost and not more than annually) to perform what are commonly called "escrow verification" services, which helps to ensure that the software and related components held in escrow are current, complete, and functional. These services can range from the very basic (and inexpensive) all the way to comprehensive (and expensive). Inventory services, the most basic, are primarily an audit of the escrow deposit to be sure what is supposed to be included is, in fact, included. Services that are more comprehensive include compile tests to validate whether the software can be recreated from the files and documentation on deposit. A full usability test is the most comprehensive verification, which confirms whether the source code in escrow is fully functional by compiling the software and then running tests on it as a part of an operational demonstration. [5] Alternatively, you have the option of requesting the service provider (at the service provider's cost and not more than annually) to have a full usability test conducted by the service provider's agent and to provide a report of the test results to you. The difference between this option and the prior option is simply one of "trust but verify," where you may want to occasionally conduct your own independent check of the service provider's check.

You also have the right to [6] go beyond traditional escrow verification services and to contract with a third-party (it could be the service provider's escrow agent if you so choose, assuming that escrow agent can provide the desired services) at your cost to provide services specific to SaaS which are intended to address and mitigate events that may or do trigger escrow. These services, for example, can include real-time replication of your data and hosting of the SaaS if you don't have the infrastructure to support it. There are a few well-known records management and backup and recovery companies specializing in SaaS recovery and data protection services that can, among other things, backup the software associated with the SaaS and your data and, if necessary, restore the software and your data.

In any case, regardless of which of the permitted choices you make, [7] the service provider is obligated to reasonably cooperate with any agent that you hire as it relates to escrow-related services. This requirement of cooperation helps to reduce any game playing or finger pointing by the service provider.

Escrow is only as good as the software and components that are deposited. If the service provider fails to provide current software to the escrow agent, the escrow provision is essentially gutted. Thus, [8] a service provider might need a strong incentive to fulfill its escrow obligations. That incentive comes in the form of remedies for you. For one, you can decide to [9] terminate the SaaS Agreement or an Exhibit A (you might decide to not terminate the SaaS Agreement and instead terminate an Exhibit A because there are other services under another Exhibit A that you want to keep) and get any prepaid fees back. In addition, you could get [10] liquidated damages in the amount of 25% of the services fees for that contract year. These liquidated damages are more than an incentive or deterrent for the service provider—the liquidated damages represent the value that you place on the service provider meeting its escrow obligations as well as the costs you'll have to absorb if there is a default and the software is unusable.

Expect much service provider hand wringing over this provision: there's not much about it a service provider will like. A service provider may take issue with the imprecise nature of "inability or unwillingness" as default events. It probably won't like the idea of a full usability test, regardless of who pays for it. It won't like the "sole election" or "sole determination" language because it gives you too much leverage. The service provider will take issue with your remedies, particularly the liquidated damages. If the services aren't that critical to you or are easily replaced, you may not need this provision at all. However, if the services are mission-critical—and that's the way this provision is written—any concession you make is likely going to impact your ability to survive the service provider going belly up.

4.   Escrow Agreement.   [1]At no additional cost to Subscriber, Service Provider agrees to place in escrow with an escrow agent copies of the most current version of the source and object code for the applicable software that is included as a part of the Services as well as all necessary components to ensure proper function of such software including but not limited to any application program interfaces, configuration files, schematics of software components, build instructions, procedural instructions, and other documentation (collectively, the "Software"). The Software shall also include all updates, improvements, and enhancements thereof from time to time developed by Service Provider and which are necessary to internally support the Services for the benefit of Subscriber. Service Provider agrees that [2]upon the occurrence of any event or circumstance which demonstrates with reasonable certainty the inability or unwillingness of Service Provider to fulfill its obligations to Subscriber in providing the Services, as determined solely by Subscriber, [3]Subscriber shall be entitled to obtain the then-current Software from the escrow agent. At the sole election of Subscriber, Subscriber shall have the right to: [4](a) perform, at Subscriber's cost and no more than annually, via a third-party escrow verification service that is independent of Service Provider and the escrow agent, a verification of Service Provider's compliance with its escrow obligations hereunder including but not limited to a full usability test of the Software; [5](b) obtain, at no additional cost to Subscriber and no more than annually, the full usability test results of the Software, such test as performed by a third-party contracted by Service Provider; and, [6](c) contract with, at Subscriber's cost, a third-party that is independent of Service Provider to perform services relating to the backup and recovery of the Services and / or Subscriber Data.   [7]Service Provider agrees to reasonably cooperate with all third-parties contracted by Subscriber for purposes of this provision. [8]Where Subscriber determines, in Subscriber's sole determination, that Service Provider has failed to fulfill its escrow obligations, Subscriber shall, at Subscriber's

sole election: [9](a) have, in addition to any other rights and remedies under this Agreement or at law, the right to immediately terminate this Agreement or the applicable <u>Exhibit A</u> and be entitled to a return of any prepaid fees; and, [10](b) be due from Service Provider twenty-five percent (25%) of the annualized Services Fees associated with the applicable <u>Exhibit A</u> for the then-current contract year as liquidated damages and not as a penalty.

Audit Rights of Service Provider

With any type of software license usage metric, be it user, hardware, or business transaction, an important consideration is asset management. Asset management as it relates to SaaS *should* be relatively easy as the software resides on a service provider's infrastructure. However, even though asset management embedded in software or SaaS is simple to implement as a technological matter, less scrupulous software licensors and service providers don't include tools to manage usage-to-metric and instead foist that burden on to the licensee or subscriber. The reason for doing so is to drive incremental revenue through compliance infractions: if the burden of asset management is on the licensee or subscriber (i.e., you) and the software doesn't have some sort of usage metering built into it, there's a good chance that a subsequent license audit will find your usage exceeding the license parameters, thereby making you liable for additional fees. That's not very nice. Thus, with any of the variations of license metrics, the responsibility for asset management is an important consideration. The SaaS Agreement side steps that consideration and impliedly assumes that the service doesn't include some sort of metering or usage governor. Instead, the language in this provision allows you to either reduce the usage or buy more capacity (at the previously agreed-upon rate, not some list price) without a penalty so as to be compliant. Preferably, however, your service provider has the ability to control usage to what your Exhibit A permits, in which case this provision isn't necessary and can be deleted from the SaaS Agreement.

[1] The service provider is *not* permitted the right to conduct an on-premises audit of your use of the services. It doesn't make sense for an on-premises audit to be conducted because the services are hosted on the service provider's infrastructure, not yours. This prohibition against on-premises audits is included in this provision because the right to conduct such audits—which doesn't make sense for SaaS—has shown up in some service providers' SaaS contract templates, likely a vestigial leftover from their traditional software licenses. Even if such audits did make logical sense for SaaS, there are a number of valid and practical reasons against permitting them. Not only is it extremely disruptive to your business operations to have a service provider on-site monkeying around in your technology infrastructure, it's also a security risk. What happens if the service provider accidently damages your hardware? Or corrupts data? Or mistakenly views data that the service provider isn't permitted to view (such as electronic protected health information)? Or introduces a virus or some other malware into your environment? Or accidentally opens up your previously secure systems to the outside world? The possibilities of something going horribly wrong are endless and very real. To protect yourself from all of the risks stemming from a service provider conducting an on-premises audit, you'd need strong indemnifications and robust remedies that go far, far beyond what are found in the typical software license agreement or in the SaaS Agreement. A service provider certainly isn't going to want to sign up to such things. Thus, the best policy is to not permit on-premises audits, whether they make logical sense or not.

Instead of an on-premises audit, [2] the service provider can, no more than annually, request that you provide a letter certifying that you haven't exceeded the number of authorized users that you contracted for. In preparing your letter, [3] if you determine you have exceeded what you contracted for, you can remedy that by either [4] reducing the number of authorized users to the contracted amount (without penalty) or [5] buy up to the number that you need (at your contracted rate and not some inflated rate). Sleazy service providers will forbid you from reducing the number of authorized users and / or will require you to pay some sort of inflated rate to buy what you need. That's a ludicrous position for a service provider to take, particularly since the service provider could have easily built a mechanism into the SaaS to meter usage rather than dumping that bogus responsibility on you. If that's the position taken by your service provider, let the service provider know that it's being ludicrous and why—you'll likely be successful in this provision going untouched.

5.   <u>Audit Rights of Service Provider</u>. [1]Service Provider shall have no right to conduct an on-premises audit of Subscriber's compliance with the use of the Services. [2]No more than once annually, Service Provider shall have the right to request from Subscriber its certification of compliance with the permitted number of Authorized Users for an <u>Exhibit A</u>. [3]Where the actual number of users exceeds the permitted number of Authorized Users, Subscriber, at Subscriber's sole election shall, within thirty (30) business days: [4](a) reduce the actual number of users so as to be in compliance with the permitted number of Authorized Users in which case no additional Services Fees shall be due to Service Provider; or, [5](b) acquire the appropriate number of Authorized Users at the rate specified in the <u>Exhibit A</u> so as to be in compliance with the permitted number of Authorized Users.

Change Control Procedure

Since circumstances and needs change, especially under a longer-term contract, it's very common for a contract to contain a change control procedure provision such as the one found in the SaaS Agreement. It's mostly straightforward. [1] Upon written notice, you have the right to request changes to the scope of the services. [2] If you request an increase in scope, within 5-business days, the service provider must tell you if there's a cost impact associated with your request. Whether there's a cost impact or not, [3] if you want the change in scope, you and the service provider are required to execute a change control to the applicable Exhibit A. It's that simple. [4]

What's not so straightforward about the provision is the very last sentence. The language of this last sentence permits you, unilaterally, to reduce scope—including the number of authorized users. For example, if the service provider objects to (and you remove) the language in the *Changes in Number of Authorized Users* provision which permits you to adjust the number of authorized users down to the minimum commitment without penalty (with a corresponding downward adjustment in your services fees), this sentence, if unchanged, provides similar flexibility and a basis for a reduction in authorized users subject to the minimum commitment described in the *Changes in Number of Authorized Users* provision. Because change control procedure provisions are so common, they don't get much scrutiny. Thus, it's very probable that a service provider won't even take notice of the last sentence. If the sentence stays in the provision, its effect can be extremely powerful and beneficial for you.

6.   <u>Change Control Procedure</u>. [1]Subscriber may, upon written notice, request changes to the scope of the Services under an <u>Exhibit A</u>. [2]If Subscriber requests an increase in the scope, Subscriber shall notify Service Provider, and, not more than five (5) business days (or other mutually agreed upon period) after receiving the request, Service Provider shall notify Subscriber whether or not the change has an associated cost impact. [3]If Subscriber approves, Subscriber shall issue a change control, which will be executed by the Service Provider. [4]Subscriber shall have the right to decrease the scope and the associated fees for an <u>Exhibit A</u> will be reduced accordingly.

Term and Termination; Renewals

This section describes the term of the SaaS Agreement as well as any corresponding Exhibit A, termination for cause and convenience, actions to be taken upon termination, and renewals (which are automatic under the SaaS Agreement). Because this section involves termination (which could afford you a lot of leverage) and renewals (which translates into service provider revenue), some of the provisions will get significant scrutiny from a service provider. Despite that, mostly, the language of the provisions in this section is relatively straightforward and innocuous, without many landmines for service providers.

Term

As previously described, the SaaS Agreement has two major components: the master agreement that contains the "legal" terms and the exhibit (Exhibit A) that contains the "business" terms. The [1] master agreement component is effective upon its effective date and is perpetual, continuing unless it's terminated for cause or convenience. An [2] Exhibit A begins on the specified start date and, unless earlier terminated for cause, terminates on the specified end date (subject to any auto-renewals). Depending on the services you contract for, you could have more than one Exhibit A, each with varying start and end dates. It's also possible that you could have no active Exhibit A, but the master agreement component is still active because it hasn't been terminated. In that case, as a practical matter, the master agreement component is "dead" even though it's still technically effective. Certainly, there are still obligations remaining between the parties such as confidentiality but essentially the master agreement component remains dormant until an Exhibit A is executed. [3] Following the initial term (i.e., at the specified end date, the Exhibit A automatically renews for a one-year period—and continues to renew every year—unless the Exhibit A is terminated for cause (for example, chronically missed services levels as provided for in the *Termination for Material and Repeated Failures* provision) or unless the Exhibit A is "actively" not renewed. To [4] stop the auto-renewal, a party (either you or the service provider) must give notice of termination at least 30-days before the end of the then-current term. The [5] termination then becomes effective on the day following the then-current term. This [3 – 5] language may not seem intuitive on first read, but the purpose is to avoid the problem of you "forgetting" to terminate in a timely manner but at the same time having the ability to terminate in a manner that is contractually acceptable to the service provider. Many subscribers lose negotiation leverage or flexibility as it relates to auto-renewals because a subscriber "forgets" to provide timely notice—while auto-renewals are easy to administer, failure to provide timely notice is the drawback and danger. This language [4] allows a very short notice period (which is an advantage because most auto-renewals require much more advance notice) but it also impliedly permits notice to be given in significant advance at a time when you remember / know / desire to terminate; for example, you could give notice a year in advance. Alternatively, you could wait until nearly the very end. To make that flexibility palatable to a service provider (if the service provider is astute enough to figure out the implied flexibility), the [5] (b) part of this provision effectively guarantees that the service provider will at least get the services fees up until what would have been the start of the next term (i.e., up to a year's worth of revenue depending on when you give notice). Ultimately, if you are uncomfortable with auto-renewals—as some subscribers are—you'll need to adjust this provision accordingly.

7.1   Term. This [1]Agreement is legally binding as of the Effective Date and shall continue until terminated as provided for herein. [2]Unless this Agreement or an Exhibit A is terminated earlier in accordance with the terms set forth herein, the term of an Exhibit A (the "Initial Term") shall commence on the Start Date and continue until the End Date. [3]Following the Initial Term and unless otherwise terminated as provided for in this Agreement, an Exhibit A shall automatically renew for successive one (1) year terms (each, a "Renewal Term") until such time as a party provides the other party with written notice of termination; provided, however, that: [4](a) such notice be given no fewer than thirty (30) calendar days prior to the last day of the then-current term; and, [5](b) any such termination shall be effective as of the date that would have been the first day of the next Renewal Term.

Termination for Convenience

Either party has the right to [1] terminate the SaaS Agreement (the master agreement component) for convenience by giving written notice to the other party [2] provided that there is no active Exhibit A. The parties don't have the right to terminate an Exhibit A for convenience, only for cause. You can, however, terminate a future term of an Exhibit A (as described in the *Term* provision). The reason behind not including Exhibit A in this provision for purposes of termination for convenience is because, to be fair and reasonable, your service provider should have some expectation of revenue assuming that it's performing well. You might be able to negotiate termination for convenience for an Exhibit A, but you'll likely have to agree to some liquidated damages for early termination as compensation for the service provider's lost revenue expectations.

If your service provider takes issue with no notice period for termination, then it doesn't understand this provision and you'll have to explain the purpose to the service provider: the provision serves a ministerial function, which is to terminate the master agreement component of the SaaS Agreement when there is no active Exhibit A.

7.2   <u>Termination for Convenience</u>. Without limiting the right of a party to terminate this Agreement or an <u>Exhibit A</u> as provided for in this Agreement, [1]a party may terminate this Agreement for convenience upon prior written notice to the other party [2]provided that there is no <u>Exhibit A</u> then in effect.

Termination for Cause

Either party has the right to [1] terminate the SaaS Agreement or a specific Exhibit A for cause [2] if the other party has materially breached the SaaS agreement (or an Exhibit A, which is part of the SaaS Agreement) and [3] the breaching party has failed to cure [4] or isn't diligent about curing within 30-days of notice of the breach. [5] The 30-day cure period doesn't apply to cases where a party has a right to immediate termination for cause (meaning, the non-breaching party doesn't need to sit around for 30-days waiting on the breaching party to cure). Immediate termination without a cure period is permitted under the following provisions: *Offensive or Disparaging Content, Changes in Functionality, Termination for Material and Repeated Failures, Escrow Agreement, Remedies for Breach of Obligation of Confidentiality, Subscriber's Right to Termination for Deficiencies.* A service provider may want to extend the cure period and may want to fiddle with the "sole satisfaction" condition to make it a lower threshold. Assuming that you retain the rights to immediate termination afforded by the provisions listed above, extending the cure period and changing the "sole satisfaction" language may be appropriate. Additionally, a service provider may want to add something to the effect that your non-payment is a cause for immediate termination without a cure period. If you agree to that, you would likely want to include language that permits such immediate termination only in the case of any undisputed payment obligation as you may have an invoice that you are, in good faith, reasonably disputing.

7.3   <u>Termination for Cause</u>. [5]Without limiting the right of a party to immediately terminate this Agreement or an <u>Exhibit A</u> for cause as provided for in this Agreement, [2]if either party materially breaches any of its duties or obligations hereunder [3]and such breach is not cured, [4]or the breaching party is not diligently pursuing a cure to the non-breaching party's sole satisfaction, within thirty (30) calendar days after written notice of the breach, the [1]non-breaching party may terminate this Agreement or an <u>Exhibit A</u> for cause as of a date specified in such notice.

Payments upon Termination

Should the SaaS Agreement or any Exhibit A be terminated, the parties need to square up on any undisputed amounts owing to the other party. This provision calls for that very thing as part of an orderly process of winding down the SaaS Agreement or an Exhibit A. A service provider likely won't have an issue with this provision, but, if the service provider is nit-picky, it may want to remove the "undisputed" language—which is unacceptable for obvious reasons.

7.4 <u>Payments upon Termination</u>. Upon the termination of this Agreement or an <u>Exhibit A</u>, Subscriber shall pay to Service Provider all undisputed amounts due and payable hereunder, if any, and Service Provider shall pay to Subscriber all amounts due and payable hereunder, such as Performance Credits and prepaid fees, if any.

Return of Subscriber Data

Under any agreement where confidential information is exchanged, a "surrender of materials" provision is nearly universally included. Under that provision, a party must either return, or certify the destruction of, the other party's confidential information. As it relates to the return of confidential information that is *not* subscriber data, the return or destruction of confidential information is addressed under the *Surrender of Confidential Information upon Termination* provision found later in the SaaS Agreement. This *Return of Subscriber Data* provision has a similar obligation of returning or destroying information, but it specifically describes the [1] disposition of subscriber (your) data upon termination. The reason for the elaboration specific to subscriber data is to address the likelihood [2] that you'll want your data back in a format that you can use, [3] that you won't want the service provider to hold your data hostage (which service providers have been known to do), and [4] that you don't want the service provider to keep a copy of it. The destruction of your data is only permitted after a copy of it has been returned to you. The reason for this qualifier is to put "delete happy" service providers on notice. Unfortunately, certain service providers have been known to accidentally (theoretically) destroy subscriber data at the end of a contract and then apologize for it when a subscriber asks for a return of its data. If that happens with this language in place, the act of destruction before return is a breach and a likely remedy would be for the service provider to rebuild your data from backups or to reimburse you for you to have that done.

A more mature and honest service provider won't have an issue with this provision other than maybe extending the period from 1-business day to a longer yet still reasonable period and / or wanting you to specify the format in advance so the service provider isn't committed to something it didn't plan for. Some number of service providers, however, will certainly [3] take issue with the language that removes any right of condition or contingency—particularly payment. That's the "hostage" part, however, and you'll need to be absolutely resolute on that point: that regardless of *anything*, the service provider *must* provide you a copy of your data. Otherwise, this provision won't have any teeth for you. Just because the service provider can't condition the extract on anything doesn't mean you won't address whatever is the basis for the service provider desire's to institute a condition (for example, on payment). It just means that the service provider will have to work it out with you and won't be able to use holding your data as hostage for leverage. [5] Since the obligation to return and / or destroy subscriber data continues past the termination of the SaaS Agreement, the provision survives termination. You'll see similar language to this provision in the *Extraction of Subscriber Data* provision further along in the SaaS Agreement.

7.5   <u>Return of Subscriber Data</u>. [1]Upon the termination of this Agreement or an <u>Exhibit A</u>, Service Provider shall, within one (1) business day following the termination of this Agreement or an <u>Exhibit A</u>, provide Subscriber, [3]without charge and without any conditions or contingencies whatsoever (including but not limited to the payment of any fees due to Service Provider), with a final extract of the Subscriber Data [2]in the format specified by Subscriber. Further, [4]Service Provider shall certify to Subscriber the destruction of any Subscriber Data within the possession or control of Service Provider but such destruction shall occur only after the Subscriber Data has been returned to Subscriber. [5]This Section shall survive the termination of this Agreement.

Renewals

Considering the high likelihood of a renewal (particularly because an Exhibit A is set up for auto-renewal), it's appropriate for you to negotiate price protection in advance and, better yet, include price reductions to reward your loyalty and to ride the service provider's downward-trending cost curve. Generally, the cost of technology decreases over time and you should be entitled to share in that. This *Renewals* provision takes a middle of the road or perhaps even a seller-centric approach in that it [1] allows the service provider to increase the "per unit" services fees by 3% per year if you haven't substantially increased your volume of business; however, it also [2] requires the service provider to lower the "per unit" services fees if you substantially increase volume.

Depending on your circumstances, this provision may require substantial modification. For example, the provision permits annual increases—if the term of the subscription is changed to, for example, 3-years, it may be necessary for you to modify the provision so that increases or decreases in services fees occur based on the term of the subscription and not annually. While some service providers are reported to have asked for 7% to 10% annual increases in services fees, increases around 3% or based on the Consumer Price Index seem to be a common and mutually agreed-upon deal point.

7.6   Renewals. Should the Services continue beyond the then-current Term, the Services Fees for the Renewal Term may be: [1](a) increased no more than three percent (3%) on an annualized per-user basis where Subscriber has not increased the number of Authorized Users by ten percent (10%) during the then-current Term; or, [2](b) decreased by no less than three percent (3%) on an annualized per-user basis where Subscriber has increased the number of Authorized Users by ten percent (10%) or greater during the then-current term.

Transition Services

A service provider benefits when its services become entrenched in a subscriber's business because entrenchment directly equates to leverage. The more entrenched a service provider becomes in your company, the greater the service provider's leverage over you and the harder it is for you to switch service providers or even insource. While some entrenchment is desired in that both parties should have some reasonable degree of commitment to each other, there is the risk that deep or broad entrenchment will dramatically inhibit your flexibility. A service provider could also become complacent and non-competitive if it's deeply entrenched in your business operations—good luck getting the service provider to step-up because the service provider knows that it's going to be tough if not nearly impossible for you to move to another service provider.

Under the SaaS Agreement, the risk of over-entrenchment and service provider dependency is mitigated through the incumbent service provider's obligation to provide transition services to a successor service provider (or to you, if you choose to insource). In short, the *Transition Services* provision works to make the transition from an incumbent service provider more orderly and, more importantly, without business disruption. The mere existence of this provision mitigates performance risk in that the service provider is aware that the leverage resulting from an entrenched relationship is diluted. Thus, the service provider has an ongoing incentive to perform under the SaaS Agreement and is keenly aware that you have the ability to terminate the SaaS Agreement and move to a successor service provider (or insource) should the incumbent service provider not satisfactorily perform its contracted obligations.

Not surprisingly, a service provider will absolutely not like the idea of this type of provision so this provision has been drafted to be generally reasonable. First, which will help your service provider get over the fact that you want this provision, the [1] service provider isn't obligated to provide transition services if the SaaS Agreement or an Exhibit A has been terminated because you haven't paid what you know you owe the service provider. Why should the service provider be obligated to help you transition the services if you're at fault for why the services need to be transitioned in the first place? Assuming you've paid up, the [2] service provider is obligated to provide you (and / or the successor service provider) with assistance that you've "reasonably" requested (you can't overreach) to transition the services in an orderly way following the termination of the SaaS Agreement or an Exhibit A. The transition services will be [3] provided on a time and materials basis. If you're concerned with what those might be in the future, you might want to try to get them nailed down and described in an Exhibit A. However, it may be hard to predict what the service provider will be providing in terms of the transition services, which is why it has been left open-ended in this provision. Whatever the cost, it's likely going to be worth it to you considering you'd be worse off with no transition services. The transition services [4] may include the services enumerated in the provision. The use of the word "may" implies that the enumerated list is not exhaustive and is only illustrative. Even so, there may be some specific services not listed here that you would want to expressly include. Obviously, [5] some sort of plan for transitioning the services would need to be developed. [6] You may also need your data to be transferred to the successor service provider. As a result of the *Return of Subscriber Data* provision, you'll get a copy of your data but your successor service provider may need a copy in a certain format that is best provided by the incumbent service provider. The incumbent [7, 8] service provider must make reasonable efforts to try to obtain the right for you to use (at your cost) any third-party [7] technology or [8] services used by the service provider to perform the services. There's no guarantee that the service provider will be successful, though, in obtaining that right for you—but at least the service provider is obligated to try. Keep in mind that the more subcontractors that are involved in providing the services the odds increase that you won't have a post-contract right to use the technology or services of a certain subcontractor. Finally, if it wasn't clear that the enumerated list is only illustrative, there's a [9] catchall for anything else that might be needed to effect an orderly transition of the services.

[10] The last substantive part of this provision might prove to be too much for your service provider to concede to, which is the ability for you to use the services for a certain period at a reduced rate if you terminated the SaaS Agreement or an Exhibit A for cause. In a way, it's reasonable because you had to terminate due to the service provider and this is a way hold the service provider accountable for that, but, in another way, it doesn't make sense because you're wanting to continue with services that were so bad that you had to terminate for cause. However, regardless of the logic, this part of the provision might be a throwaway when you're bartering for something else.

[11] Since the obligation to provide transition services continues past the termination of the SaaS Agreement and because some of the provisions of the SaaS Agreement will continue to apply (such as payment to the service provider for the transition services), this provision and applicable provisions of the SaaS Agreement survive termination.

8.   Transition Services. [1]Provided that this Agreement or an Exhibit A has not been terminated by Service Provider due to Subscriber's failure to pay any undisputed amount due Service Provider, [2]Service Provider will provide to Subscriber and / or to the service provider selected by Subscriber (such service provider shall be known as the "Successor Service Provider") assistance reasonably requested by Subscriber to effect the orderly transition of the Services, in whole or in part, to Subscriber or to Successor Service Provider (such assistance shall be known as the "Transition Services") following the termination of this Agreement or an Exhibit A, in whole or in part. The [3]Transition Services shall be provided on a time and materials basis and [4]may include: [5](a) developing a plan for the orderly transition of the terminated Services from Service Provider to Subscriber or Successor Service Provider; [6](b) if required, transferring the Subscriber Data to Successor Service Provider; [7](c) using commercially reasonable efforts to assist Subscriber in acquiring any necessary rights to legally and

physically access and use any third-party technologies and documentation then being used by Service Provider in connection with the Services; [8](d) using commercially reasonable efforts to make available to Subscriber, pursuant to mutually agreeable terms and conditions, any third-party services then being used by Service Provider in connection with the Services; and, [9](e) such other activities upon which the parties may agree. Notwithstanding the foregoing, [10]should Subscriber terminate this Agreement or an Exhibit A due to Service Provider's material breach, Subscriber may elect to use the Services for a period of no greater than six (6) months from the date of termination at a reduced rate of twenty (20%) percent off of the then-current Services Fees for the terminated Services. [11]All applicable terms and conditions of this Agreement shall apply to the Transition Services. This Section shall survive the termination of this Agreement.

Fees and Expenses

The *Fees; Billing* section of the SaaS Agreement is mostly limited to the mechanics of how and when payment is due and made, but, as you might expect, this section tends to get well-warranted scrutiny from service providers because it involves money. The provisions in this section of the SaaS Agreement are what service providers typically see from subscriber-to-subscriber and the language is mostly innocuous. However, there are some points of contention and other items worth worthy of expanded discussion in this section. Exhibit A dictates the billing frequency. With SaaS, it's typical to price on a per-user per-month basis, but then be billed quarterly or annually.

9.   Fees; Billing. Subscriber shall be responsible for and shall pay to Service Provider the fees as further described in an Exhibit A, subject to the terms and conditions contained in this Agreement and such Exhibit A. Any sum due Service Provider for the Services for which payment is not otherwise specified

shall be due and payable thirty (30) business days after receipt by Subscriber of an invoice from Service Provider.

Billing Procedures

There isn't anything particularly interesting or controversial about this provision, but you will need to tailor it to your company's accounts payable practices. The provision assumes a [1] hardcopy invoice is required for payment. You will also need to [2] include the method by which your company intakes invoices for payment.

9.1   Billing Procedures.   Unless otherwise provided for under an Exhibit A, Service Provider shall bill to Subscriber the sums due pursuant to an Exhibit A by Service Provider's invoice, which shall contain: (a) Subscriber's purchase order number, if any, and Service Provider's invoice number; (b) description of Services for which an amount is due; (c) the fees or portion thereof that are due; (d); taxes, if any; (e); any Performance Credits or other credits; and, (f) total amount due.   Service Provider shall forward invoices in [1]hardcopy format to [2][Subscriber Accounts Payable Address].

Credits

There isn't anything controversial about this provision, but it's noteworthy to point out that you have the option of obtaining any performance credit as a [1] credit against fees or an [2] actual payment to you.

9.3   Credits.   Any amounts due to Subscriber, such as a Performance Credit, from Service Provider [1]may be applied by Subscriber, at the sole election of Subscriber, against any current or future fees due to Service Provider.   [2]Any such amounts that are not so applied by Subscriber shall be paid to Subscriber by Service Provider within thirty (30) calendar days following Subscriber's request.   This Section shall survive the termination of this Agreement.

Non-Binding Terms

This provision is essentially a "battle of the forms" provision. Battle of the forms most commonly refers to situations where contracting parties, at offer and acceptance, exchange conflicting forms and, in the event of a dispute, leave a court to resolve which form is the governing form. The battle can also occur between a buyer and a seller who are beyond the offer and acceptance stage, have entered into a written contract, and then exchange purchase orders and invoices that contain incompatible terms and conditions. All sorts of legal jargon and esoteric analyses apply when a battle of the forms occurs; for example, the "mirror image" and "last shot" rules. Rather than having to train and prepare for battle, the best option—at least with contracts—is to seek a peaceful truce. That's accomplished through this *Non-Binding Terms* provision. The provision is bolstered by the *Entire Agreement* provision, which states that the SaaS Agreement (and any attachments such as an Exhibit A) constitute the entire agreement between you and the service provider and that the SaaS Agreement can only be amended by an instrument in writing that has been signed by both parties—rather than by, for example, pre-printed forms exchanged between the parties.

9.4   <u>Non-binding Terms</u>. Any terms and conditions included in a Subscriber purchase order or a Service Provider invoice, as the case may be, shall be deemed to be solely for the convenience of the respective party, and no such term or condition shall be binding upon the parties.

Auditable Records

[1] Service providers are accustomed to subscribers requesting that records relating to fees billed and fees paid be retained and made available for audit by a subscriber. The requirements of the first part of the *Auditable Records* provision are extremely commonplace and likely won't present an issue for a service provider. [2] The second part of the provision might give a service provider some pause, primarily because it involves audit reporting that has only been in

place since 2011 and that goes far beyond traditional financial auditing.

The American Institute of Certified Public Accountants (AICPA) Service Organization Control (SOC) 1 type 1 and type 2 reports, SOC 2 type and type 2 reports, and SOC 3 report replaced and extended the Statement on Auditing Standards 70 (SAS 70) in 2011. SAS 70 was the de facto standard for data center customers to assure themselves that their data center service provider had effective internal controls in place for managing the design, implementation, and execution of customer information. SAS 70 consisted of type I and type II audits. The type I audit was designed to assess the sufficiency of the service provider's controls as of a particular date and the type II audit was designed to assess the effectiveness of the controls as of a certain date. A SAS 70 audit only verified that the controls the service provider had in place were followed. There was no minimum bar that a service provider had to achieve and there was no standard to hold service providers accountable. A service provider with weak controls could claim the same level of audit as a service provider with strong controls. The only way a customer could tell the difference was to read through the detailed audit report. The other problem with SAS 70 was that it was never designed to be used by service providers that offer colocation or clouding computing (such as SaaS).

SOC 1 reports are performed in accordance with Statement on Standards for Attestation Engagements (SSAE) 16, Reporting on Controls at a Service Organization. SOC 1 reports focus solely on controls at a service provider that are likely to be relevant to an audit of a subscriber's financial statements. SOC 2 and SOC 3 reports are performed in accordance with Attestation Standards, Section 101 of the AICPA Codification Standards (AT Section 101). SOC 2 and SOC 3 reports address controls of the service provider that relate to operations and compliance.

As with SAS 70, SOC 1 reports are available as a type 1 or type 2 report. A SOC 1 type 1 report presents the auditors' opinion regarding the accuracy and completeness of management's description of the system or service as well as the suitability of the design of controls as of a specific date. A SOC 1 type 2 report includes the type 1 criteria and audits the operating effectiveness of the controls throughout a declared period, generally between 6-months and 1-year.

SOC 2 reporting was specifically designed for cloud computing, SaaS, and IT managed services service providers. A SOC 2 report (either type 1 or type 2) is similar to a SOC 1 report in scope and content but a SOC 2 report specifically addresses any number of the five so-called "Trust Services Principles," which are: Security (the system is protected against unauthorized access, both physical and logical); Availability (the system is available for operation and use as committed or agreed); Processing Integrity (system processing is complete, accurate, timely, and authorized); Confidentiality (information designated as confidential is protected as committed or agreed); and, Privacy (personal information is collected, used, retained, disclosed, and disposed of in conformity with the commitments in the service provider's privacy notice, and with criteria set forth in Generally Accepted Privacy Principles issued by the AICPA).

SOC 3 reporting also uses the Trust Services Principles but provides only the auditor's report on whether the system achieved the specified principle (and doesn't contain the detail a SOC 2 report does). A key difference between a SOC 2 report and a SOC 3 report is that a SOC 2 report is generally a restricted-use report because of the detail it contains and a SOC 3 report is a general-use report because it's not as detailed. A good use of a SOC 3 report would be for prospective subscribers of a service provider as a marketing tool and a SOC 2 report would be reserved for existing subscribers who need to, for example, verify compliance to contractual obligations of information security.

Another way of looking at the differences between SOC 1, SOC 2, and SOC 3 is to consider the audience of the various reports: your external auditors who audit your company's financial statements will be interested in the SOC 1 report, your IT staff will be interested in the SOC 2 report, and prospective subscribers of the service provider may be interested in the SOC 3 report.

[2] Most subscribers require their service provider to undergo the type 2 report examination for the greater level of assurance it provides, therefore, this provision requires that type for SOC 1 and SOC 2. For the SOC 2 report, the service provider is required to provide an examination of all Trust Services Principles (Security, Availability, Processing Integrity, Confidentiality, and, Privacy). A SOC 3 report is not required since it's essentially a mere summary of what is contained in a SOC 2 report and is more of a marketing tool.

9.5   Auditable Records. [1]Service Provider shall maintain accurate records of all fees billable to, and payments made by, Subscriber in a format that will permit audit by Subscriber for a period of no less than three (3) years from when a fee was incurred or a payment was made. The foregoing obligation of Service Provider shall survive the termination of this Agreement. For the term of this Agreement, [2]upon Subscriber's written request, Service Provider shall provide Subscriber with a copy of its annual American Institute of Certified Public Accountants Service Organization Control (SOC) 1 type 2 report and SOC 2 type 2 report (for all Trust Services Principles).

Billing Reviews by Third-Parties

In managed services agreements for technology-related services, particularly those that are long-term (or have the potential to be long-term), the parties occasionally include a "market check" type of provision that allows the buyer to review and compare its current billing against the competitive marketplace. Surprisingly, sellers are mostly agreeable to these types of provisions because they help to avoid a future competitive bid. Rather than risk the buyer going through a competitive bidding process, which may cost the incumbent seller the buyer's business, the incumbent seller agrees to a review of its pricing as compared to the competitive market and, if there's a difference favorable to the buyer, the seller adjusts its pricing to the buyer. It's a win-win. The buyer gets the benefit of better pricing and doesn't have to transition to a new seller. The seller keeps the business and retains a profit margin that is consistent with the competitive marketplace. Sellers that take issue with this type of provision are either clueless, shortsighted, or ripping you off. If your service provider is any one of those, you'll hear a multitude of objections as to why this provision doesn't make sense, is unfair, unreasonably impacts the service provider's profit margin, and so on. More astute service providers will be accommodating but will likely want to modify this provision so that it's specific to your subscription, more precise in its application of who performs the review, or perhaps bounded in terms of fee adjustments.

9.6   <u>Billing Reviews by Third-Parties</u>. For purposes of determining the competitiveness and appropriateness of fees charged to Subscriber by Service Provider, Subscriber is entitled to disclose to a third-party this Agreement, any <u>Exhibit A</u>, and any other data pertaining to fees paid or payable by Subscriber to Service Provider.

No Suspension of Services

It's reasonable for a service provider to be diligent about being paid for the services it provides, but it's not reasonable for a service provider to use a threat of suspending services when there's a valid reason you haven't yet paid. Unfortunately, history has shown that some service providers behave like mob enforcers and will threaten to suspend—or actually do suspend—services if a subscriber doesn't cough up payment even when the subscriber has a valid reason for not paying (such as the service provider screwed up an invoice). Service providers have also been known to destroy subscriber data for non-payment.

This provision permits you to reasonably dispute an invoice or—because some accounts payable departments get busy—be reasonably late on paying an invoice. With that said, this provision isn't something you should rely on often. If you have invoicing problems, escalate that early and often with the service provider. If you have a slow accounts payable department, see what you can do to get that department back on track. Part of being a good customer is paying on time.

9.7   <u>No Suspension of Services</u>. Service Provider shall not suspend any part of the Services where: (a) Subscriber is reasonably disputing any amount due to Service Provider; or, (b) any unpaid but undisputed amount due to Service Provider is less than ninety (90) business days in arrears.

Representations and Warranties

As indicated by the title, this section contains representations and warranties of the parties. There are two provisions comprising this section: mutual representations and warranties and those made only by the service provider. Expect significant scrutiny of this section by a service provider. As indicated further in the discussion of this section, a number of the representations and warranties are intended for you to spot issues and raise discussion with a service provider.

The terms "representation" and "warranty" are frequently used interchangeably even though they have very different meanings. Not that you need to be a legal expert on the difference in meanings—it's a trivial point until there's a contract dispute and only then will it matter in helping to determine your remedy. A representation is made at a point in time; essentially, a one-time inducement to enter into a contractual relationship. Failure of a representation to be true is generally a breach of contract. If the false representation is material, it could result in the right to rescind the contract under a claim for fraud.

A warranty is an ongoing promise that a certain fact (or set of facts) will be true. A warranty can be for a set period of time, such as a date certain, or can be indefinite. If the fact of the warranty becomes untrue during the period of the warranty, there is a breach of contract. A warranty is conclusively presumed to be material. With a representation, the party claiming breach has the burden to show that the representation is material. As opposed to a remedy of rescission for the breach of a representation, the remedy for breach of warranty is a cure or to be made whole (e.g., a refund of monies paid). Usually, under a warranty, one party is responsible for a warranty to another party, although certain warranties can be reciprocal. A warranty can be of two types: express (written in the contract) or, depending on the nature of the transaction, implied (*not* written in the contract). Under a commercial sale of goods transaction, the UCC creates the implied warranties of merchantability, fitness for particular purpose, and non-infringement. A UCC implied warranty can be expressly disclaimed by the use of specific language in a contract provided that the disclaimer is conspicuous (e.g., capitalized letters). One way to think about the UCC implied warranties is that they reverse the "buyer beware" rule and chiefly serve to protect a buyer.

The implied warranty of merchantability requires that goods purchased by a buyer from a seller conform to ordinary standards of care and that they are of the same average grade, quality, and value as similar goods sold under similar circumstances. For the warranty to apply, the goods must be something that the seller normally sells and the goods must be used by the buyer for the good's ordinary purpose. The policy behind this implied warranty is that sellers are generally better suited than buyers to determine whether goods are proper. Holding the seller liable for goods that are not fit for the ordinary purpose for which the goods are intended shifts the costs of nonperformance from the buyer to the seller. This motivates the seller to ensure the goods' proper performance before placing the goods on the market. The policy behind limiting the implied warranty of merchantability to the goods' ordinary use is straightforward: a seller may not have sufficient expertise or control over goods to ensure that the goods will perform properly when used for nonstandard purposes.

Fitness for particular purpose applies if the seller knows or has reason to know that the buyer will be using the goods for a certain purpose; if so, the seller impliedly warrants that the goods being sold are suitable for that specific purpose. The rationale behind this warranty is that buyers typically rely on a seller's skill and expertise to help them find the specific goods that meet the buyers' specific need. It's unfair for a seller to sell goods that the seller knows will not meet the needs of the buyer and then later tell the buyer it isn't the seller's fault that the goods didn't work for the buyer's particular purpose. Unlike the implied warranty of merchantability, the implied warranty of fitness for particular purpose does not contain a requirement that the seller be a merchant with respect to the goods sold.

Under an implied warranty of non-infringement, if the seller regularly deals in the goods sold, the seller must hold the buyer harmless against any rightful claim of infringement by a third-party. The reasons for this warranty are basic: to deter sellers from selling goods they don't have a right to sell or to profit from goods that infringe upon some third-party's intellectual property rights.

Mutual

The representations and warranties (actually, mostly representations) in the *Mutual* provision of the *Representations and Warranties* section are generally of the benign boilerplate type. **[1]** Depending on your geographical use of the SaaS and the location of your data and from where the services are being provided (the SaaS Agreement assumes U.S. only), you may want to add "international" to the compliance with laws warranty. The last sub-provision, a representation, **[2]** is an issue spotter. If a service provider is currently engaged in litigation that may impact its business, the service provider will likely have heartburn with this representation. If a service provider expresses concern over the representation, it's your opportunity to probe for more information. With that information, you can decide what the risk is for you, if any.

10.1   Mutual. Each of Subscriber and Service Provider represent and warrant that:

   10.1.1   it is a business duly incorporated, validly existing, and in good standing under the laws of its state of incorporation;

   10.1.2   it has all requisite corporate power, financial capacity, and authority to execute, deliver, and perform its obligations under this Agreement;

10.1.3 the execution, delivery, and performance of this Agreement has been duly authorized by it and this Agreement constitutes the legal, valid, and binding agreement of it and is enforceable against it in accordance with its terms, except as the enforceability thereof may be limited by bankruptcy, insolvency, reorganizations, moratoriums, and similar laws affecting creditors' rights generally and by general equitable principles;

10.1.4 it shall comply with all applicable federal, state, local, [1]or other laws and regulations applicable to the performance by it of its obligations under this Agreement and shall obtain all applicable permits and licenses required of it in connection with its obligations under this Agreement; and,

10.1.5 [2]there is no outstanding litigation, arbitrated matter or other dispute to which it is a party which, if decided unfavorably to it, would reasonably be expected to have a potential or actual material adverse effect on its ability to fulfill its obligations under this Agreement.

By Service Provider

Unlike the prior provision, with its mutuality and mostly nonthreatening language, this provision's powerful representations and warranties are made exclusively by the service provider for your benefit. It's unlikely that a service provider will make it through this provision without raising at least one major issue with the language because of the strong degree of commitment that it places on the service provider. The language by no means is unreasonable or one-sided: each of the representations or warranties is something that a qualified service provider is fully capable of making—and should make. A service provider's willingness to do so is a different matter.

Referring back to the implied warranties of the UCC, those implied warranties only apply to a transaction involving the sale of goods and not for services. As it relates to software licenses, courts have gone both ways—but in a very fact specific manner—and have found that software is and is not a good. SaaS hasn't yet been fully tested in the courts for purposes of determining whether the UCC's implied warranties apply, but, based on prior legal cases determining whether software is a good or a service, it's highly likely that SaaS would be found to be a service and not a good. Regardless, SaaS service providers, in their contract templates, routinely disclaim all of the UCC implied warranties—which means that service providers are either fearful of the implied warranties possibly applying to SaaS or they're just being sloppy by including contract language that doesn't apply. If you believe that a service provider includes a disclaimer of implied warranties out of fear that they may apply, it really doesn't matter if the implied warranties ultimately do apply. Assuming a dispute with a service provider, long before you ever make it to a courtroom for a determination as to whether one or more implied warranties apply, you'll likely come to a settlement with the service provider. For that duration prior to the settlement, the service provider will likely continue to believe the implied warranties apply— and you'll continue to have that leverage over the service provider. In that way, there's an argument for avoiding a disclaimer of the implied warranties: the mere potential of implied warranties applying gives you possible leverage in a dispute with a service provider. As explained below, one tricky way of avoiding a disclaimer of the implied warranties by a service provider involves illusion and a sleight of hand of sorts.

This *By Service Provider* provision of the *Representations and Warranties* section contains an express version of the UCC implied warranties. Under the implied warranty of merchantability, the UCC Section 2-314 requires that the [1] seller be a "merchant with respect to goods of that kind," meaning the kind of goods the seller usually sells in the marketplace. A seller does not make an implied warranty of merchantability when it sells goods of a kind that the seller does not normally sell. Assuming that the seller does normally sell the goods, [2] the goods must be reasonably fit for the ordinary purposes for which such goods are used.

When a buyer wishes to use goods for a particular, non-ordinary purpose, the UCC Section 2-315 provides an implied warranty of fitness for particular purpose. The UCC merely requires that the [3, 4] seller possess knowledge and expertise on which the buyer may rely. The implied warranty of fitness for particular purpose [5] applies if the seller knows or has reason to know that the buyer will be using the goods for a specific purpose. If the seller knows the specific purpose for which the goods are to be used, the seller impliedly warrants that the goods being sold are suitable for that particular purpose.

Under the implied warranty of title and against infringement, which is commonly referred to as the implied warranty of non-infringement, the UCC Section 2-312 states that [1] "a seller that is a merchant regularly dealing in goods of the kind" warrants that the seller has the [6] legal right to transfer the goods and that the [7] goods don't infringe the intellectual property rights of some third-party. If there is a non-frivolous claim of infringement made by a third-party against the buyer that adversely impacts the buyer's use of the goods, the seller must hold the buyer harmless against the claim.

Thus, to summarize, this provision of the SaaS Agreement contains an express affirmation of the three UCC implied warranties. This is where the illusion and sleight of hand come in: a service provider will occasionally recognize the implied warranties in their express form, realize the potent nature of the warranties, and then strike them from your SaaS Agreement. Because the service provider is not operating from its contract template, it makes assumptions, doesn't understand certain non-obvious but powerful interconnections between contract language, and fails to recognize what's missing from the SaaS Agreement that would be beneficial to the service provider. The "what's missing" part is the most critical part of any contract review, and requires much more expertise and thoughtful analysis than merely modifying or deleting what has already been laid out before you as contract language to review. What's missing from the SaaS Agreement is a disclaimer of warranties. In order for the UCC implied warranties to *not* be implied in a contract, the UCC requires that the warranties be disclaimed in a conspicuous and specific writing. While such a disclaimer is very likely to be in a service provider's contract template, it's quietly absent from the SaaS Agreement. After the service provider strikes the "express" implied warranties from your SaaS Agreement, more often than not, the service provider moves on in its contract review and fails to include the required disclaimer. As a result, even though the "express" implied warranties in your SaaS Agreement were struck, as an operation of law, you still have the warranties because they're implied in your contract. The foregoing might seem to be an unwholesome tactic, but you can bet that the contract template your service provider uses on a regular basis has similar landmines.

Under a contract, when there is a breach, the parties have fashioned or will fashion some sort of remedy to compensate for the breach. Torts are civil wrongs other than breaches of contracts, for which the law provides a remedy. Although separate bodies of law, there is strong interplay between contract law and the tort of negligence. This tort occurs when one of the contracting parties (the "tortfeasor") has a duty of care and, through the tortfeasor's actions or inactions, violates the standard of care that is owed to the other party and that other party is subsequently harmed. Negligence differs from intentional torts in that it doesn't require that a tortfeasor intentionally desire to harm the other party—all that must initially occur is a violation of a duty that the one party owed to the other party. That, in turn, means a duty and standard of care should be established in a contract. In the SaaS Agreement, the bar for the standard of care is set high: [4] "expert" and [9] "highest professional standards." It's possible that a service provider will attempt to lower the standard to "reasonable" or "consistent with industry standards." Whether that's appropriate or not depends on the SaaS to which you're subscribing. If it's a common service, such as email, for which your data isn't sensitive, a lower standard may be acceptable to you. The presence of some harm (damages) is generally a necessary part of a tort claim. Thus, it's not enough to demonstrate that you have suffered a wrong in order to win a tort case, you must also have legally recognized damages that were directly or indirectly caused by the tortfeasor as a result of the tort, and you must be able to prove the extent of those damages. [4] It's helpful, but not conclusive, to point out to a potential tortfeasor the foreseeability of damages that could result from any negligence.

Under case law, courts in the U.S., including the Supreme Court have implied a warranty of "workmanlike" performance in certain contracts. This implied warranty has mostly applied to construction or related services: should a seller fail to deliver a service that conforms with standards due to latent defects, the buyer has a legal remedy, as accepted and defined by a history of cases, and in some instances, by law. The rationale for the warranty is that a sophisticated seller is in a better position than a buyer, who is unable to control the service being provided, to recognize and assess latent problems before they arise. That [9] same rationale can be creatively extended to any sort of service as an express warranty, including SaaS. Thus, in this provision, the service provider is required to expressly warrant that it will be subject to a "workmanlike" standard of performance This is in addition to the other standards of performance also described in this provision that are used for the purposes of potentially needing to establish a tort claim of negligence.

Courts can award a buyer various types of contract damages under a buyer-seller contract, such as restitution interest (seller caused losses and must return buyer's money) and expectancy interest (seller prevented gains and must give the value of what the buyer expected). Sometimes a contracting party may suffer a loss or have a gain prevented due to reliance on something that was appropriately assumed but not itemized in a contract. The doctrine of detrimental reliance is an equitable theory of recovery, and its purpose is to afford a party relief even if a contract isn't express or specific as to the parties' obligations of performance. To prevail on a claim for detrimental reliance, a party must prove three elements: a representation by conduct or word, justifiable reliance, and a change in position to one's detriment because of the reliance. [4] To that end, this provision includes an express affirmation of your reliance on the service provider and the possibility of your damages based on that reliance.

It's beneficial—but not always neatly practical—in a contract to have the logical sequence of: (a) representation or warranty; (b) promise; and, (c) remedy. That holds true for non-infringement. Even without considering the implications of the implied warranty of non-infringement, the obligation of non-infringement is made clearer by a [6] representation by the service provider that it has the right to provide the services and a [7] warranty by the service provider that the services are non-infringing. This clarity helps to avoid any question as to the service provider's obligation of the remedy described in the *Proprietary Rights Indemnification* provision. A service provider will likely want to limit the [7] warranty of non-infringement to existing U.S. intellectual property rights at the time the SaaS Agreement was executed. This change—assuming that it's carried through to the *Proprietary Rights Indemnification* provision—could adversely and materially impact your remedies in the case of an infringement claim by limiting indemnification only to U.S. intellectual property rights that arose prior to, or at the time of, the SaaS Agreement. This change is unreasonable because, rather than making it your problem, the service provider should have conducted sufficient due diligence in foreign jurisdictions to protect against claims of infringement and the service provider should have perfected its intellectual property rights to deter future claims of infringement.

As a means to help avoid any claims of infringement, the [8] service provider warrants that it will disclose to you any third-party intellectual property required by the service provider in the performance of the services and that the service provider will have valid written agreements with any such third-parties for the use of their intellectual property. This warranty also serves as an issue spotter for you: if the service provider has a myriad patchwork of third-parties it's relying on to perform the services, you have at least that many points of failure and potential problems. This warranty is rarely an issue for a service provider because it needs the protection as much as you do.

Less "legal" than the prior representations and warranties is the [10] warranty that the service provider will ensure that no viruses unintentionally disrupt your technology environment and the [11] representation that no mechanisms will intentionally disrupt your use of the services. [10] If the service provider does introduce a virus into your technology environment, the service provider is required to reimburse you for your costs (including the cost of your staff's time) to get rid of the virus and to get back to the same place where you were before the virus was introduced. Service providers will occasionally try to lower the standard from "best efforts" to "reasonable efforts" and / or balk at having to pay your costs of virus removal and recovery. That response from a service provider serves as an issue spotter for you and allows you to question the service provider as to its security practices. If your data is sensitive, the unwillingness of a service provider to use its best efforts to stop viruses from being introduced into its environment and yours should be deeply concerning and cause you to consider whether you have the right service provider. [11] With traditional software licensing, certain (and more unscrupulous) licensors built hidden mechanisms in their software that could be accessed through a secret "trap door." If you were late on a payment or did something else the licensor didn't like, the licensor could magically—and without warning—shut your software off by triggering the self-help disabling mechanism. The disabling mechanism, when triggered, occasionally corrupted a licensee's data. Since, under a traditional software license, the software resided on the licensee's technology infrastructure, significant ingenuity was required to create the hidden disabling mechanism and the secret trap door. That ingenuity is not required for SaaS. SaaS sits on the service provider's infrastructure and the service provider doesn't need to worry about secret trap doors—the service provider, in essence, just triggers a disabling mechanism in its environment if it doesn't want you to use the services any longer. To help protect you from that, but it's no guarantee that it won't happen, the service provider represents that the services don't have a disabling mechanism. If it turns out your service provider was confused and a disabling mechanism did exist which corrupted your data, the service provider would have to remedy any loss of your data. To further bolster that the service provider won't disable your use of the services without due cause, the [12] service provider warrants that it won't stop you from using the services and won't hold your data hostage if you're reasonably disputing an invoice that you haven't yet paid. Mostly, disabling mechanisms have disappeared and nearly every service provider permits its subscribers to reasonably dispute invoices, so the representation of no disabling mechanism and the warranty of not shutting off the services due to an invoice dispute are rarely an issue for a service provider.

Lastly, [13] so that you can have some reasonable reliance that the services will perform in the way that the service provider's documentation says the services will and in the way that the mutually agreed-upon description of the services (the Exhibit A) says the services will, the service provider warrants so. Service providers don't take issue with this warranty because it only requires *material* conformance of the services to the documentation and an Exhibit A (versus complete or total conformance).

10.2   <u>By Service Provider</u>. Service Provider represents and warrants that:

    10.2.1 [1]it is in the business of providing the Services;

    10.2.2 [2]the Services are fit for the ordinary purposes for which they will be used;

    10.2.3 [3]it is possessed of superior knowledge with respect to the Services;

    10.2.4 [4]it acknowledges that Subscriber is relying on its representation of its experience and expert knowledge, and that any substantial misrepresentation may result in damage to Subscriber;

10.2.5 [5]it knows the particular purpose for which the Services are required by Subscriber;

10.2.6 [6]it is the lawful licensee or owner of the Services (excluding any Subscriber Data therein) and has all the necessary rights in the Services to grant the use of the Services to Subscriber;

10.2.7 [7]the Services and any other work performed by Service Provider hereunder shall not infringe upon any United States or foreign copyright, patent, trade secret, or other proprietary right, or misappropriate any trade secret, of any third-party, and that it has neither assigned nor otherwise entered into an agreement by which it purports to assign or transfer any right, title, or interest to any technology or intellectual property right that would conflict with its obligations under this Agreement;

10.2.8 [8]it shall disclose any third-party (which shall, for purposes of this Agreement, be deemed a subcontractor) whose intellectual property is incorporated into the Services or who is necessary for the performance of the Services and it shall maintain in-force written agreements with such third-party, if any, for the term of the applicable Exhibit A;

10.2.9 [9]it has the expertise to perform the Services in a competent, workmanlike, and professional manner and in accordance with the highest professional standards;

10.2.10 [10]it will use its best efforts to ensure that no computer viruses, malware, or similar items (collectively, a "Virus") are introduced into Subscriber's computing and network environment by the Services, and that, where it transfers a Virus to Subscriber through the Services, it shall reimburse Subscriber the actual cost incurred by Subscriber to remove or recover from the Virus, including the costs of persons employed by Subscriber;

10.2.11 [11]the Services are free of any mechanism which may disable the Services and Service Provider warrants that no loss of Subscriber Data will result from such items if present in the Services;

10.2.12 [12]in the case of Subscriber's reasonable dispute of any Service Provider invoice, it shall not withhold the performance of Services, including, without limitation, access and use of the Services, Technical Support, Maintenance, and extract of Subscriber Data; and,

10.2.13 [13]the Services will conform in all material respects to the specifications, functions, descriptions, standards, and criteria set forth in the applicable Exhibit A and the Documentation.

Subscriber Data

With a traditional computing environment, you have complete control over your data. You can invest as much or as little as desired to protect and retain your data. Even if you outsourced your data center, you still have a great degree of control—at least within the perimeter network. With SaaS, your data is "out there, somewhere" traversing the badlands of the Internet. Corresponding with the steady migration of data to the Internet, an alphabet soup of government agencies, regulations, and standards has come to a full boil, subjecting companies to a bewildering array of data protection and privacy, information security, and record retention requirements; to name but a few: Children's Online Privacy Protection Act (COPPA), Fair Credit Reporting Act (FCRA), Financial Industry Regulatory Authority (FINRA), Gramm-Leach-Bliley Act (GLBA),

Health Information Technology for Economic and Clinical Health Act (HITECH), Health Insurance Portability and Accountability Act (HIPAA), Sarbanes–Oxley Act (SOX). That list doesn't include the myriad of state laws, which may also apply. Failing to comply with regulations and standards subjects your company to fines (financial risk), and, worse, your company being on the front page of the newspaper (reputational risk).

In the SaaS Agreement, data protection and privacy, information security, and record retention are predominately addressed in this *Subscriber Data* section and the *Data Privacy and Information Security* section. Subscriber data, as explained later, is also controlled by the *Non-Disclosure of Confidential Information* section. Collectively, these sections define what comprises your data, set the standard of care, describe the obligations of the service provider relating to your data, specify procedures for the parties to follow, create your rights of service provider oversight and monitoring, and lay out a plethora of remedies.

The SaaS Agreement assumes a data classification of "personally identifiable information" or "PII." In brief, PII is information that can be used to uniquely identify an individual or can be used with other sources to uniquely identify an individual. Examples of that information include full name, social security number or other government-issued identification number, date of birth, address, and telephone number. The District of Columbia, every U.S. territory, and almost every state have enacted legislation specific to data protection / privacy and notification of security breaches. The states that haven't yet will. Data protection and information security is an area of state—and federal—law that is continually (and quickly) evolving: every new, well-publicized loss of data will likely result in some new law or an amendment of an existing law. A subscriber in a highly regulated industry should carefully review the laws and regulations that it may be subject to in order to ensure that the SaaS Agreement and the obligations of the contracting parties comply with any data protection and privacy, information security, and record retention requirements. Arguably, you could rely on the warranty of compliance with laws contained in the *Representations and Warranties –*

Mutual provision and the general obligation contained in the *Compliance with Laws; Subscriber Policies and Procedures* provision. It's not, however, a prudent solution to place all of the burden of figuring out the what, when, and how of regulatory compliance on the shoulders of your service provider.

Massachusetts passed a data protection law that is one of the most stringent in the nation (at the time of this book's publication). This law (201 CMR 17.00) mandates that "every person who owns, licenses, stores or maintains personal information about a resident of the Commonwealth [of Massachusetts] shall be in full compliance with 201 CMR 17.00." It requires companies with PII to have an adequate protective system in place to prevent unauthorized access to the PII, firewall and malware protection for the computer systems, as well as encryption for all data containing PII transmitted through a public network or wirelessly.

The SaaS Agreement, through this section and the *Data Privacy and Information Security* section, contractually implements what would be required of a subscriber to be compliant with the intent of the most stringent state laws. As previously indicated, state law relating to data protection and privacy is continuing to evolve. Once you've executed a SaaS Agreement with a service provider, it's practically a certainty that the contract language relating to data protection and privacy will, at some point, be outdated or made obsolete by new and changed laws. However, don't let that possibility alarm you—the provisions contained in this *Subscriber Data* section, the warranty of compliance with laws contained in the *Representations and Warranties – Mutual* provision, and the *Data Privacy and Information Security* section do not relieve or protect a service provider from the requirement to comply with laws as they're enacted or amended. Compliance with laws that a service provider (or a subscriber) is subject to is an absolute and that is made clear by the warranty of compliance with laws contained in the *Representations and Warranties – Mutual* provision and the general obligation of compliance under the *Compliance with Laws; Subscriber Policies and Procedures* provision. Thus, even if the contract language becomes outdated or obsolete relating to data privacy and information security, current law—and the SaaS Agreement—requires ongoing compliance.

While the SaaS Agreement assumes your data will contain PII and contains appropriate contract language to that effect, the contract language is also applicable to protecting traditional "confidential" information such as company financials and the like. Thus, if your data won't include PII but will include confidential business information, you will only need to make minor changes to this section and the *Data Privacy and Information Security* section to exclude PII. There are other, and sometimes higher, levels of data classification protected under industry standards or under federal law (versus just state law). For example, cardholder data under the Payment Card Industry (PCI) Data Security Standard and electronic protected health information under HIPAA. If you have other data classifications that require a higher level of data privacy and information security, you will need to revise this section and the *Data Privacy and Information Security* section as appropriate.

Ownership

Before describing who owns the subscriber data, the *Ownership* provision describes what the subscriber data consists of. Defining subscriber data clearly and with specificity removes any ambiguity and makes it clear that you have the final say—including demanding an extract—over what happens with and to your data. In this provision, subscriber data is defined as any data relating to the subscriber that is **[1]** "collected, used, processed, stored, or generated" as a part of your use of the services, **[2]** such data to include any PII. The provision **[3]** mandates specific treatment of your data by classifying it as confidential information. As a result, in addition to this section's descriptions of how the service provider is to use and handle your data, the service provider is also subject to all of the conditions and obligations described in the *Non-Disclosure of Confidential Information* section. With what constitutes your data now being clearly defined, the language is clear through its simplicity: **[4]** the data is yours solely and exclusively, and all ownership ("right, title, and interest") is vested in you with no ownership rights being transferred to or shared with the service provider. Even though no one other than an individual truly "owns" his or her PII, for purposes of the SaaS Agreement and who does what with the PII, that data is considered subscriber data. Your service provider is basically a custodian—or perhaps even a fiduciary—of your data, but it is not the "owner." [5] Since it's possible—and likely—that a service provider will continue to hold your data after the expiration of the SaaS Agreement until it's returned to you or destroyed, this provision (i.e., who owns the data) survives the termination of the SaaS Agreement.

Service providers rarely take issue with the ownership of data being vested in the subscriber, but a service provider may take issue with the categorical classification of your data as confidential information. Instead, a service provider may want to disconnect the two, having separate obligations. This position will likely be the case if your data isn't sensitive or doesn't have attributes that would normally constitute confidential information.

11.1   <u>Ownership</u>.   Subscriber's data ("Subscriber Data," which [3]shall also be known and treated by Service Provider as Confidential Information) shall include: [1](a) Subscriber's data collected, used, processed, stored, or generated as the result of the use of the Services; and, [2](b) personally identifiable information ("PII") collected, used, processed, stored, or generated as the result of the use of the Services, including, without limitation, any information that identifies an individual, such as an individual's social security number or other government-issued identification number, date of birth, address, telephone number, biometric data, mother's maiden name, email address, credit card information, or an individual's name in combination with any other of the elements listed herein. [4]Subscriber Data is and shall remain the sole and exclusive property of Subscriber and all right, title, and interest in the same is reserved by Subscriber. [5]This Section shall survive the termination of this Agreement.

Service Provider Use of Subscriber Data

With ownership of subscriber data established, the service provider is [1] granted a limited license to your data for the purpose of providing the services. That license to use the subscriber data comes with certain restrictions as well as a standard of care. The service provider is required to [2] treat subscriber data as confidential, consistent with the *Non-Disclosure of Confidential Information* section, and must use a standard of care in accordance with the treatment of confidential information, other obligations relating to subscriber data under the SaaS Agreement (for example, the *Data Privacy and Information Security* section), and any applicable law so as to avoid any loss of the data. Consistent with the limited license, the service provider agrees that [3] it will only use subscriber data for the sole and exclusive purpose of providing the services and that its use will be in accordance with the SaaS Agreement, the applicable Exhibit A, and any applicable law. [4] Finally—even though "solely and exclusively" is clear enough—the service provider agrees that it won't use subscriber data for its or anyone else's benefit unless you otherwise agree. As with the other provisions in this *Subscriber Data* section, [5] since the service provider may have your data following the termination of the SaaS Agreement, this provision survives such termination.

This provision is mostly reasonable to a service provider, but, as with this *Subscriber Data* section in general, the service provider may not like the references to "applicable law" and will want the specific laws named—and, if not, the service provider isn't responsible. That position isn't reasonable as laws are added and changed over time, and, secondly, the service provider is subject to the law as is anyone else and, in most cases, won't be able to shield itself from the law by contracting around it.

11.2   Service Provider Use of Subscriber Data. Service Provider is provided a [1]limited license to Subscriber Data for the sole and exclusive purpose of providing the Services, including a license to collect, process, store, generate, and display Subscriber Data only to the extent necessary in the providing of the Services.

Service Provider shall: [2](a) keep and maintain Subscriber Data in strict confidence, using such degree of care as is appropriate and consistent with its obligations as further described in this Agreement and applicable law to avoid unauthorized access, use, disclosure, or loss; [3](b) use and disclose Subscriber Data solely and exclusively for the purpose of providing the Services, such use and disclosure being in accordance with this Agreement, the applicable Exhibit A, and applicable law; and, [4](c) not use, sell, rent, transfer, distribute, or otherwise disclose or make available Subscriber Data for Service Provider's own purposes or for the benefit of anyone other than Subscriber without Subscriber's prior written consent. [5]This Section shall survive the termination of this Agreement.

Extraction of Subscriber Data

As explained earlier under the *Return of Subscriber Data* provision, some service providers have held subscriber data hostage in order to have leverage over the subscriber. With that provision, the service provider is required to provide you with an extract of your data when the SaaS Agreement or an Exhibit A is terminated. Ideally, the SaaS that you're subscribing to provides you with the ability to self-extract a full copy of your data, but, if not, you're dependent on the service provider to make that happen. To cover any situation other than at termination, the *Extraction of Subscriber Data* provision requires the service provider to give you an extract of your data. This extract must occur [1] within 1-business day of your request and [2] must be in the format you specify. The service provider [3] can't condition the extract or make it contingent on anything, including payment of any amounts then due to the service provider. Even so, taking a "belt and suspenders" approach, the service provider specifically represents and warrants in the *Representations and Warranties – By Service Provider* provision that it shall not withhold providing you with an extract of your data if the service provider hasn't been paid but you're disputing (reasonably) an invoice.

As with the *Return of Subscriber Data* provision, most service providers won't have an issue with this provision other than maybe extending the period from 1-business day to a longer yet still reasonable period and / or wanting you to specify the format in advance. However, depending on the nature of your business, a longer timeframe may not be acceptable: if you're in an industry subject to frequent legal holds and discovery orders, access to your data in a timely manner is critical. As previously explained, [3] certain service providers will balk at not being able to condition the extract on anything. Again, that's the precise purpose of this provision: to remove your data as a point of leverage for the service provider for every silly little disagreement that comes along. You'll just have to stand firm on the no "conditions or contingencies" part of this provision. It should be a deal-breaker for you because, if a service provider does insist on conditioning an extract of your data, it tells you that the service provider will use your data as leverage against you. If the service provider is worried about, for example, payment, it has other remedies and rights at law and doesn't need to hold your data hostage.

11.3   <u>Extraction of Subscriber Data</u>. Service Provider shall, [1]within one (1) business day of Subscriber's request, provide Subscriber, without charge and [3]without any conditions or contingencies whatsoever (including but not limited to the payment of any fees due to Service Provider), an extract of the Subscriber Data in the [2]format specified by Subscriber.

Backup and Recovery of Subscriber Data

In a traditional computing environment, backup and recovery of data is under your control—you decide how much or little risk you're willing to absorb. With SaaS, if you're not precise in contracting your backup and recovery requirements, you could be giving up more control over your data than desired or intended. In addition to internal policies that your company may have regarding record retention, you could also be subject to complying with certain regulations that mandate record retention. The *Backup and Recovery of Subscriber Data* provision takes a middle-of-the-road approach but, depending on your record retention requirements, the service provider's obligations may be excessive or may be wholly inadequate. If you're in a highly regulated industry, you may even decide to have another service provider—one specializing in the backup and recovery of critical subscriber data in SaaS environments—perform the services, which would preclude the need for this provision.

Included [1] as a part of the services—implying no additional cost—the service provider has the general obligation to maintain a backup of your data such that it can be recovered on a timely basis. This obligation of the service provider is a continuing one: the *Force Majeure; Excused Performance* provision specifically excludes backup and recovery from any force majeure event. The [2] general nature of the obligation is more specifically defined to be a real-time or "contemporaneous" backup and a 2-hour recovery time. If you're contracting for multiple different services under the SaaS Agreement, you can modify that default by describing different backup and recovery requirements in an Exhibit A. [3] On a daily basis, the service provider must store your data off-site at a facility that is constructed, i.e., "hardened," to protect your data against loss. That facility, whether owned by the service provider or contracted to a third-party, is subject to the security requirements described in the *Data Privacy and Information Security* section. [4] A cost that subscribers are frequently surprised by is the data storage fees associated with backups. This language is intended to do two things: (a) to send a message to the prospective service provider who is reviewing the SaaS Agreement as a part of your competitive bidding process that you don't intend on paying anything more for backup and recovery; and, (b) to help you spot the issue if there is a hidden fee for backup and recovery.

11.4   Backup and Recovery of Subscriber Data. [1]As a part of the Services, Service Provider is responsible for maintaining a backup of Subscriber Data and for an orderly and timely recovery of such data in the event that the Services may be interrupted. [2]Unless otherwise described in an Exhibit A, Service Provider shall maintain a contemporaneous backup of Subscriber Data that can be recovered within two (2) hours at any point in time. Additionally, Service Provider shall [3]store a backup of Subscriber Data in an off-site "hardened" facility no less than daily, maintaining the security of Subscriber Data, the security requirements of which are further described herein. Any [4]backups of Subscriber Data shall not be considered in calculating storage used by Subscriber.

Loss of Data

While the *Backup and Recovery of Subscriber Data* provision obligates the service provider to take measures that have the effect of lessening the impact of any loss of your data, it's not a contractual remedy. What happens if your data is lost? What if the security of PII is inadvertently breached and the data is exposed? That's where this *Loss of Data* provision comes in—it provides you with a multitude of remedies if there is a suspected or actual loss of data. As you review the remedies in this provision, keep in mind that you have additional remedies in the SaaS Agreement that may not be immediately obvious. Under the *Non-Disclosure of Confidential Information* section, since your data is also classified as confidential information, you have the right to seek injunctive relief against any breach of your data and you have the right to immediately terminate the SaaS Agreement or an Exhibit A. Under the *Data Privacy and Information Security* section, the service provider is required to implement any safeguards that you identify to prevent any future loss of data. You should carefully review the remedies contained in this *Loss of Data* provision to ensure that you have all of the remedies necessary for the nature of your data.

The remedies are [1] triggered if there is any suspected or actual loss of subscriber data [2] due to essentially anything the service provider did, didn't do, should have done, or could have done. The remedies are [3] also triggered if there was no suspected or actual loss of subscriber data but the physical, technical, administrative, or organizational safeguards put in place by the service provider that relate to subscriber data were either suspected to be compromised or actually were compromised. [4] All of the remedies aren't necessarily triggered—only the remedies that apply to the occurrence are triggered. A service provider may not like the degree of liability imposed by this provision and may want to limit the circumstances that trigger the remedies to gross negligence and willful misconduct. However, it's appropriate for you to shift to the service provider some of the liabilities associated with the financial and reputational harm that could result from a loss of data. Unfortunately, for service providers, the responsibilities and corresponding liabilities of managing subscriber data come along with the profits of their SaaS offerings. As much as a service provider might wish otherwise and want to divorce any liabilities from its responsibilities, it's hard for a service provider to argue that it shouldn't be accountable for the loss or breach of your data.

When the service provider [5] becomes aware of a suspected or actual loss of data or compromise of safeguards, it's required to notify you within 24-hours. It must then [6] cooperate with you in investigating the occurrence, which includes making certain information and materials available to you as may be required by law or as you otherwise require. In the event of a recalcitrant service provider, the contractual obligation to cooperate is particularly helpful. [7] In the case of PII, at your option, the service provider must [8] notify the affected individuals as soon as reasonably possible but no later than when the law requires or, if no law applies, within 5-days. A service provider may argue that the 5-day period is insufficient and that it needs a longer timeframe. The length of the timeframe may be a legitimate issue if you only have mailing addresses for the affected individuals or not an issue if you have the ability to provide notification via email. Your [9] other option is for you to make the notification and for the service provider to reimburse you the cost of notification. Depending on the extent of the loss of data and who's affected, you may want to take on the responsibility of notification to be assured that all that can be done is being done. A service provider may balk at this—it will either want its costs associated with your notification to be capped or it won't want you to have the option of notification.

It's becoming common under state law and industry practices for credit and identity monitoring services to be offered to individuals affected by a loss of data. The [10] service provider is required to provide such services (via contracting with a third-party) where there is an occurrence related to PII and the services must be provided for as long as what the law requires or, if no law applies, for 12-months. [11] As a catchall, the service provider must do whatever else is required by applicable law. A service provider won't like the general, open nature of this remedy and will likely seek to make it more specific or will want to strike it completely. Ultimately, whether the service provider likes it or not—and whether or not this particular remedy stays in the SaaS Agreement—the service provider *is* responsible to do what the law requires. [12] In a "belt and suspenders" fashion, a specific indemnification is included. The indemnification is practically identical to the *General Indemnification* provision. A service provider may argue that this indemnification is duplicative—and it would be right. The reason it's included here is based on the possibility that, during contract negotiations, the *General Indemnification* provision becomes watered-down. If that's the case and this duplicative indemnification remains unchanged, you would have the indemnification needed for this specific situation. If the *General Indemnification* provision remains unchanged and the service provider wants this particular indemnification language struck from the SaaS Agreement, that's a reasonable and acceptable request.

Depending on the nature of the loss, [13] an actual loss of your data may require recreating the data—which the service provider is responsible for, based on your schedule and without charge. A service provider will likely agree to the "without charge" part of the remedy but may want to base the schedule on the service provider's timeframe.

To ensure that a suspected or actual loss doesn't occur again, the service provider [14] must provide to you, within 10-days, a plan that contains all of the actions the service provider will undertake to prevent a future loss. As with the prior remedy, a service provider may want to expand the timeframe to develop the plan. Finally, [15] in the case of PII and should you opt to have the service provider make the notification to affected individuals, the notification must contain the elements described in this provision.

These elements are a combination of those required by state and federal laws, but may be made obsolete or insufficient by new or changed laws. Thus, the language includes the requirement that the notification "comply with applicable law." This provision [16] survives the termination of the SaaS Agreement so as to include any situations where the service provider still has your data following contract termination or where the loss occurs just prior to termination and the service provider hasn't yet fulfilled the remedies required under this provision.

11.5   <u>Loss of Data</u>. [2]In the event of any act, error or omission, negligence, misconduct, or breach that [1]compromises or is suspected to compromise the security, confidentiality, or integrity of Subscriber Data or the [3]physical, technical, administrative, or organizational safeguards put in place by Service Provider that relate to the protection of the security, confidentiality, or integrity of Subscriber Data, Service Provider shall, [4]as applicable: [5](a) notify Subscriber as soon as practicable but no later than twenty-four (24) hours of becoming aware of such occurrence; [6](b) cooperate with Subscriber in investigating the occurrence, including making available all relevant records, logs, files, data reporting, and other materials required to comply with applicable law or as otherwise required by Subscriber; [7](c) in the case of PII, at Subscriber's sole election, [8](i) notify the affected individuals who comprise the PII as soon as practicable but no later than is required to comply with applicable law, or, in the absence of any legally required notification period, within five (5) calendar days of the occurrence; or, [9](ii) reimburse Subscriber for any costs in notifying the affected individuals; [10](d) in the case of PII, provide third-party credit and identity monitoring services to each of the affected individuals who comprise the PII for the period required to comply with applicable law, or, in the absence of any legally required monitoring services, for no less than twelve (12) months following the date of notification to such individuals; [11](e) perform or take any other actions required to comply with applicable law as a result of the occurrence; [12](f) without limiting Subscriber's obligations of indemnification as further described in this Agreement, indemnify, defend, and hold harmless Subscriber for any and all Claims (as defined herein), including reasonable attorneys' fees, costs, and expenses incidental thereto, which may be suffered by, accrued against, charged to, or recoverable from Subscriber in connection with the occurrence; [13](g) be responsible for recreating lost Subscriber Data in the manner and on the schedule set by Subscriber without charge to Subscriber; and, [14](h) provide to Subscriber a detailed plan within ten (10) calendar days of the occurrence describing the measures Service Provider will undertake to prevent a future occurrence. [15]Notification to affected individuals, as described above, shall comply with applicable law, be written in plain language, and contain, at a minimum: name and contact information of Service Provider's representative; a description of the nature of the loss; a list of the types of data involved; the known or approximate date of the loss; how such loss may affect the affected individual; what steps Service Provider has taken to protect the affected individual; what steps the affected individual can take to protect himself or herself; contact information for major credit card reporting agencies; and, information regarding the credit and identity monitoring services to be provided by Service Provider. [16]This Section shall survive the termination of this Agreement.

Non-Disclosure of Confidential Information

Practically relegated to the category of boilerplate, non-disclosure and confidentiality provisions in buyer-seller contracts are typically very mundane and non-controversial. However, with the SaaS Agreement, there are some nuances in the provisions contained in this section that merit some further explanation.

By virtue of the survival clause contained in this section, the parties' duty to hold in confidence any confidential information that was disclosed during the term of the SaaS Agreement shall remain in effect indefinitely. If you would rather have a finite period, you could replace the survival clause with something to the effect of "The parties' duty to hold in confidence the Confidential Information disclosed during the Initial Term or any Renewal Term shall remain in effect for a [fill in the time period of months or years] period following the termination of this Agreement."

Meaning of Confidential Information

As with many confidentiality provisions, this provision defines confidential information to be [1] anything marked confidential (or marked something similar, such as "sensitive" or "proprietary") or [2] anything that wasn't marked confidential or indicated to be confidential but was later summarized in writing and marked as confidential (or something similar). Confidential information is [3] also defined to be anything the receiving party should have reasonably known to be confidential information of the disclosing party. That definition is obviously somewhat vague and broad, and allows the disclosing party to make the claim after unauthorized disclosure that the receiving party should have known better. If you're the one likely to be the receiving party most of the time, you may take issue with that definition, but, in the context of your being a subscriber, it's more likely the receiving party will be the service provider. Service providers occasionally realize that and strike this definition, which if struck, is probably a reasonable concession for you to make.

Another common part of a confidentiality provision is what confidential information *isn't*. The common exclusions are found here in this provision. Confidential information doesn't include: [4] any information of the disclosing party in the possession of the receiving party that the receiving party already had without an obligation of confidentiality; [5] any information independently developed by the receiving party that the receiving party can show it developed without doing anything untoward; [6] any information obtained by the receiving party that the receiving party obtained from another party without an obligation of confidentiality; and, [7] any information that was or becomes publicly available (that the receiving party didn't make publicly available in an unauthorized manner). [8] In the case of your data, it's *always* treated as confidential information for purposes of the SaaS Agreement regardless of [1 – 3] any of the inclusions or [4 – 7] any of the exclusions.

12.1   Meaning of Confidential Information. For the purposes of this Agreement, the term "Confidential Information" shall mean all information and documentation of a party that: [1](a) has been marked "confidential" or with words of similar meaning, at the time of disclosure by such party; [2](b) if disclosed orally or not marked "confidential" or with words of similar meaning, was subsequently summarized in writing by the disclosing party and marked "confidential" or with words of similar meaning; and, [3](c) should reasonably be recognized as confidential information of the disclosing party. The term "Confidential Information" does not include any information or documentation that was: [4](a) already in the possession of the receiving party without an obligation of confidentiality; [5](b) developed independently by the receiving party, as demonstrated by the receiving party, without violating the disclosing party's proprietary rights; [6](c) obtained from a source other than the disclosing party without an obligation of confidentiality; or, [7](d) publicly available when received, or thereafter became publicly available (other than through any unauthorized disclosure by, through, or on behalf of, the receiving party). For purposes of this Agreement, [8]in all cases and for all matters, Subscriber Data shall be deemed to be Confidential Information.

Obligation of Confidentiality

The obligation of confidentiality for each of the parties is to: [1] not disclose any confidential information [2] to anyone other than those who have a need to know in connection with the SaaS Agreement; [3] to not use any confidential information for any purposes other than the performance of the SaaS Agreement; and, [4] to advise others to keep the information confidential.

12.2   <u>Obligation of Confidentiality</u>. [1]The parties agree to hold all Confidential Information in strict confidence and not to copy, reproduce, sell, transfer, or otherwise dispose of, give or disclose such Confidential Information to [2]third parties other than employees, agents, or subcontractors of a party who have a need to know in connection with this Agreement or to [3]use such Confidential Information for any purposes whatsoever other than the performance of this Agreement. [4]The parties agree to advise and require their respective employees, agents, and subcontractors of their obligations to keep all Confidential Information confidential.

Cooperation to Prevent Disclosure of Confidential Information

Not only does the receiving party have an obligation to not disclose any confidential information of the disclosing party, the [1] receiving party also must use its best efforts to identify and prevent the unauthorized use or disclosure of the disclosing party's confidential information. That includes [2] advising the disclosing party if the receiving party believes or knows that someone with access to the confidential information has violated or will violate the confidentiality of that information. [3] To help prevent or stop a violation, the receiving party must cooperate with the disclosing party in taking legal action, such as seeking an injunction.

Because the SaaS Agreement is subject to U.S. law, your PII is subject to the Uniting and Strengthening America by Providing Appropriate Tools Required to Intercept and Obstruct Terrorism Act—better known as the USA PATRIOT Act. The Act was passed in 2001 following the September 11th attacks on the World Trade Center in New York City to help fight terrorism and money laundering activities as well as to provide certain additional investigative powers to U.S. law enforcement officials. These additional investigative powers make it easier for law enforcement officials to intercept electronic communications and business records. Under certain exceptions, law enforcement officials have the right, using a type of subpoena called a National Security Letter, to seize subscribers' PII held by service providers without a court order, regardless of where in the world the data is stored. The Act also gives law enforcement officials the right to prevent service providers from informing subscribers that their subscriber data was seized. Regardless, some subscribers append this type of provision to state that cooperation includes subscriber notification by the service provider of the seizure of confidential information or subscriber data by any U.S. law enforcement agency, where such notification of the subscriber by the service provider is not otherwise prohibited by law.

12.3   Cooperation to Prevent Disclosure of Confidential Information. [1]Each party shall use its best efforts to assist the other party in identifying and preventing any unauthorized use or disclosure of any Confidential Information. Without limiting the foregoing, [2]each party shall advise the other party immediately in the event either party learns or has reason to believe that any person who has had access to Confidential Information has violated or intends to violate the terms of this Agreement and [3]each party will cooperate with the other party in seeking injunctive or other equitable relief against any such person.

Remedies for Breach of Obligation of Confidentiality

If there is a breach of confidentiality, the non-breaching party's first action is to stop the breaching party from continuing to disclose confidential information. [1] The way to "stop" that continuing breach is for the non-breaching party (the "complainant") to march off to the courthouse to seek an injunction. An injunction is an equitable remedy in the form of a court order that requires a party to do or refrain from doing specific acts (like disclosing confidential information). A party that fails to comply with an injunction faces penalties and may have to pay damages. [2] For a complainant to receive an injunction, the complainant must show it has suffered irreparable harm and that no other remedy for the wrong is adequate or complete. To aid in that showing, it's common for contracts that include confidentiality obligations, such as the SaaS Agreement, to include a provision in which the parties acknowledge that a breach of confidentiality will cause irreparable harm and that the complainant will be entitled to injunctive relief to enforce any breach or threatened breach of confidentiality. That showing is also bolstered by damages associated with a breach of confidentiality being excluded from the *Limitation of Liability* provision (meaning that the potential amount of damages is unlimited). While such contractual acknowledgments may be a factor in the award of an injunction, they're unlikely to be dispositive: they don't actually establish irreparable harm or entitle a party to an injunction. As an equitable remedy, an injunction involves the exercise of a court's discretion, and a court will likely require persuasive evidence of irreparable harm.

As another remedy, you (as the subscriber) reserve the unilateral right to [3] immediately terminate the SaaS Agreement or an Exhibit A without liability should the service provider threaten to breach or actually breach its obligation of confidentiality. There might be situations where you elect to continue with the services if the service provider breaches confidentiality and there might be situations that you want to get out of the SaaS Agreement completely or parts of it (via terminating an Exhibit A). Since the remedy is unilateral, it's likely that a service provider will ask that it be made mutual since the obligation of confidentiality is mutual.

12.4   <u>Remedies for Breach of Obligation of Confidentiality</u>. [2]Each party acknowledges that breach of its obligation of confidentiality may give rise to irreparable injury to the other party, which damage may be inadequately compensable in the form of monetary damages. Accordingly, [1]a party may seek and obtain injunctive relief against the breach or threatened breach of the foregoing undertakings, [3]in addition to any other legal remedies which may be available, to include, in the case of Subscriber, at the sole election of Subscriber, the immediate termination, without liability to Subscriber, of this Agreement or any <u>Exhibit A</u> corresponding to the breach or threatened breach.

Surrender of Confidential Information upon Termination

It's common for a receiving party to have an obligation to [1] return or [2] destroy confidential information of the disclosing party that is still in the possession of the receiving party. This provision is typical but some customization of it was necessary for the SaaS Agreement since subscriber data is included as a part of confidential information. [3] The return and destruction of subscriber data is governed by the *Return of Subscriber Data* provision so subscriber data is therefore expressly excluded from this provision.

12.5 <u>Surrender of Confidential Information upon Termination</u>. Upon termination of this Agreement or an <u>Exhibit A</u>, in whole or in part, each party shall, within five (5) calendar days from the date of termination, [1]return to the other party any and all Confidential Information received from the other party, or created or received by a party on behalf of the other party, which are in such party's possession, custody, or control; [3]provided, however, that Service Provider shall return Subscriber Data to Subscriber following the timeframe and procedure described further in this Agreement. Should Service Provider or Subscriber determine that the return of any non-Subscriber Data Confidential Information is not feasible, such party shall [2]destroy the non-Subscriber Data Confidential Information and shall certify the same in writing within five (5) calendar days from the date of termination to the other party.

Data Privacy and Information Security

A chief concern of companies considering the use of SaaS has centered on data privacy and information security and how well a service provider can protect data. Your due diligence relating to "how well" should be thoroughly conducted during the competitive bidding and service provider qualification / evaluation process—but the result of that due diligence should show up in this provision in the form of contract language. What the service provider said its data privacy and information security capabilities are during due diligence need to be supported by corresponding language in this provision. If there's any disconnect between the two or the service provider materially pushes back on what you include in this provision, *caveat emptor!*

Where the *Subscriber Data* and *Non-Disclosure of Confidential Information* sections go more to the legal and logical protections of your data (and information), the *Data Privacy and Information Security* section more narrowly focuses on the physical, technical, administrative, and organizational safeguards—a data privacy and information security program—put in place by the service provider. Broadly, security goes to who can access the data whereas privacy goes to what can be done with the data once access is authorized. While the contract language contained in the SaaS Agreement and the explanation of that language in this book assumes common, prudent data privacy and information security standards in the context of the continental U.S., this book is not intended to be a treatise on information security and data privacy. Caution: no matter what comprises your data or where your data is located, it's imperative that you conduct additional and appropriate research to ensure that your SaaS Agreement with the service provider sufficiently addresses your specific situation.

Although not required by this *Data Privacy and Information Security* section, there are a number of standards, assessments, and certifications specific to cloud computing and SaaS that you may want to include as being required to follow, attain, or maintain. Most recently, the following appear to leading the herd: Cloud Security Alliance's Cloud Controls Matrix (CCM); Information Systems Audit and Control Association's Control Objectives for Information and Related Technology (COBIT); Federal Risk Authorization and Management Program (FedRAMP); CloudeAssurance; European Network and Information Security Agency's Cloud Computing Risk Assessment. CCM, COBIT, and FedRAMP are highlighted in the following paragraphs.

One of the more robust cloud security frameworks is the Cloud Security Alliance's CCM, consisting of security control requirements built for the cloud. The CCM is specifically designed to provide fundamental security principles to guide cloud service providers and to assist prospective subscribers in assessing the overall security risk of a service provider. The framework emphasizes information security control requirements and identifies security threats and vulnerabilities in the cloud. The CCM also aligns with industry-accepted security standards and controls frameworks such as the International Organization for Standardization (ISO) and the International Electrotechnical Commission (IEC) 27001/270021 (a model for establishing, reviewing, and improving an information security management system), Information Systems Audit and Control Association's (ISACA) COBIT, PCI, and the National Institute for Standards and Technology (NIST), among others.

ISACA's COBIT is a risk and controls framework, developed as a tool to map business requirements to IT controls for managing and securing information and information systems. That framework was extended to cloud computing: ISACA's IT Control Objectives for Cloud Computing. These control objectives map to other industry-accepted security standards, regulations, and controls frameworks such as NIST Special Publication 800-53 Rev. 3 Recommended Security Controls for Federal Information Systems and Organizations, ISO 17799: Information Technology – Security Techniques – Code Of Practice For Information Security Management, and the Capability Maturity Model Integration (CMMI), among others.

The U.S. Government established FedRAMP to provide a standard approach to assessing and authorizing cloud computing services and products. This approach leverages the existing processes based on NIST Special Publication 800-37 Guide for Applying the Risk Management Framework to Federal Information Systems Processes and the NIST Special Publication 800-53 Rev. 3 Recommended Security Controls for Federal Information Systems and Organizations, adapting them for cloud computing. FedRAMP offers a repeatable security assessment process—instead of having a cloud service provider undergo an assessment for each potential government agency subscriber, FedRAMP lets a service provider go through one evaluation that can be used multiple times. If your service provider provides SaaS under a government contract, it may have gone through this assessment.

If you do elect to require any one of the foregoing or any other standard, assessment, or certification, there's one near-certainty: because of the emerging and conflicting standards and certifications, subscribers will struggle with determining what is the most applicable to their needs.

Undertaking by Service Provider

[1] In addition to the service provider's obligation of confidentiality under the *Non-Disclosure of Confidential Information* section, the service provider is required to have a data privacy and information security program that covers the gamut from physical security to organizational safeguards. The program must [2] secure your data, [3] protect it against any foreseeable threats or hazards, [4] protect it against unauthorized disclosure, use, or access, and [5] ensure that it is disposed of properly. [6] The program must also include procedures that require compliance by those working on behalf of the service provider. [7] Since no third-party standard applies— which you can easily add to this provision based on your needs—*your* security program is the benchmark. However, if your security program isn't robust, you may not want to use it as a standard for purposes of the SaaS Agreement.

13.1   <u>Undertaking by Service Provider</u>. [1]Without limiting Service Provider's obligation of confidentiality as further described herein, Service Provider shall be responsible for establishing and maintaining a data privacy and information security program, including physical, technical, administrative, and organizational safeguards, that is designed to: [2](a) ensure the security and confidentiality of the Subscriber Data; [3](b) protect against any anticipated threats or hazards to the security or integrity of the Subscriber Data; [4](c) protect against unauthorized disclosure, access to, or use of the Subscriber Data; [5](d) ensure the proper disposal of Subscriber Data; and,

[6](e) ensure that all employees, agents, and subcontractors of Service Provider, if any, comply with all of the foregoing. [7]In no case shall the safeguards of Service Provider's data privacy and information security program be less stringent than the safeguards used by Subscriber.

Audit by Service Provider

Based on the nature of your data, the SOC 2 report described in the *Auditable Records* provision may be inadequate as an audit for purposes of evaluating the completeness and effectiveness of the service provider's data privacy and information security program. The *Audit by Service Provider* provision requires the service provider to conduct an audit on an annual basis that is specific to its data privacy and information security program and to provide the findings to you.

13.2　Audit by Service Provider.　No less than annually, Service Provider shall conduct a comprehensive independent third-party audit of its data privacy and information security program and provide such audit findings to Subscriber.

Right of Audit by Subscriber

[1] To evaluate the completeness and effectiveness of the service provider's data privacy and information security program, the *Right of Audit by Subscriber* provision gives you the right to audit the service provider at any time prior to the start of the services or during the performance of the services. [2] During the performance of the services, your right to conduct an on-site audit (at your expense) can be exercised at any time without notice to the service provider. You're not limited to the type of audit, and, relating to data privacy and information security, there are many different types: for example, architecture reviews, minimum security baselines, external vulnerability scans, external penetration tests, PCI gap assessments, HIPAA gap assessments. You also have the [3] option, in lieu of an on-site audit, to require the service provider to respond to a questionnaire within the specified timeframe. This isn't a

questionnaire that you develop on the fly—it's a formalized questionnaire that you buy or license, the service provider completes, and a composite result is derived. There are many different organizations that provide the questionnaires and there are many different questionnaires specific to cloud computing: for example, the Shared Assessments Program, Cloud Security Alliance's Consensus Assessments Initiative Questionnaire (CAIQ), CloudeAssurance.

It's highly likely that a service provider is going to have heartburn with this provision. Just like you not wanting the service provider to conduct an on-premises audit to assess your use of the services, a service provider doesn't want to be subject to the same invasiveness. A service provider also won't like your right to conduct an audit anytime you want without notice. It will also want to limit the scope of the audit. Expect significant modification of this provision or a complete strike of it by a service provider. If you have highly sensitive data and represent a big chunk of business to the service provider, you might have enough leverage to keep the provision intact. Otherwise, if you manage to at least have the audit questionnaire obligation kept in the SaaS Agreement, consider yourself to have done well.

13.3   Right of Audit by Subscriber. Without limiting any other audit rights of Subscriber, [1]Subscriber shall have the right to review Service Provider's data privacy and information security program prior to the commencement of Services and from time to time during the term of this Agreement. [2]During the providing of the Services, on an ongoing basis from time to time and without notice, Subscriber, at its own expense, shall be entitled to perform, or to have performed, an on-site audit of Service Provider's data privacy and information security program. [3]In lieu of an on-site audit, upon request by Subscriber, Service Provider agrees to complete, within forty-five (45 days) of receipt, an audit questionnaire provided by Subscriber regarding Service Provider's data privacy and information security program.

Audit Findings

This is a small but powerful provision that can prove to be contentious during negotiations. It requires the service provider to implement *any* safeguards that you or any audit identifies relating to the service provider's data privacy and information security program. There's no mutual agreement as to what safeguards are truly important or required, no limit on the cost, and no discussion of timeframe to implement. A service provider may ask for some or all of those things to be added to this provision. A service provider may also want to remove you as one who identifies safeguards and limit such identification to qualified third-parties. In fairness, this provision is heavily weighted to the subscriber and placing some limiting parameters around the language could be reasonable.

13.4 <u>Audit Findings</u>. Service Provider shall implement any required safeguards as identified by Subscriber or by any audit of Service Provider's data privacy and information security program.

Subscriber's Right to Termination for Deficiencies

The safeguarding of your data is paramount and the failure of a service provider to fulfill its obligations in that regard is an inexcusable and material breach. Therefore, you have the right to terminate the SaaS Agreement or an Exhibit A without liability if the service provider doesn't fulfill its obligations under this *Data Privacy and Information Security* section by not having an adequate data privacy and information security program, not conducting or allowing privacy or security audits, or not implementing audit recommendations or your recommendations. A service provider may not like your right to terminate so easily and may want to strike this language, but remember that your most critical asset is your data and it must be protected. If the service provider isn't doing that (and it's not as if the service provider didn't know that data protection was important to you), you need the ability to terminate. The language requires a reasonableness standard in making the determination of the service provider's failure to perform, so the provision isn't as one-sided as it may initially seem. A service provider may also want a cure period, but that's not appropriate if the service provider is bleeding your data all over the Internet. It's also not appropriate because, in all likelihood, you got to this provision only after audits identified the deficiencies and the service provider failed to correct them. Therefore, in essence, the service provider already had a cure period. As painful as it might be for you to suddenly shut down your use of the SaaS, it's not nearly as painful as responding to reporters' or a government investigator's questions regarding deficiencies related to the privacy and security of your data. That's a scenario that your company might not ever recover from. And that's why you need the right to immediately terminate and that's why this provision is worth fighting hard for.

13.5   Subscriber's Right to Termination for Deficiencies. Subscriber reserves the right, at its sole election, to immediately terminate this Agreement or an Exhibit A without limitation and without liability if Subscriber reasonably determines that Service Provider fails or has failed to meet its obligations under this Section.

Proprietary Rights

This section is relatively straightforward, infrequently an issue, and doesn't require much detailed explanation. Essentially, the language says, "what's yours is yours" and "what's mine is mine." A service provider may want to beef up the *Pre-existing Materials* provision or may want it more specific.

Keep in mind that the definition of confidential information includes subscriber data. If that definition is somehow changed to not include subscriber data, you're still protected against the service provider somehow inferring ownership of your data by virtue of the *Ownership* provision in the *Subscriber Data* section.

14.1   Pre-existing Materials. Subscriber acknowledges that, in the course of performing the Services, Service Provider may use software and related processes, instructions, methods, and techniques that have been previously developed by Service Provider (collectively, the "Pre-existing Materials," which shall include the Services) and that the same shall remain the sole and exclusive property of Service Provider.

14.2 <u>No License</u>. Except as expressly set forth herein, no license is granted by either party to the other with respect to the Confidential Information or Pre-existing Materials. Nothing in this Agreement shall be construed to grant to either party any ownership or other interest, in the Confidential Information or Pre-existing Materials, except as may be provided under a license specifically applicable to such Confidential Information or Pre-existing Materials.

14.3 The provisions of this Section shall survive the termination of this Agreement.

Indemnification; Liability; Insurance

While words like "indemnification," "liability," and "insurance" may sound like a lot of legalese, they're worth paying attention to since they can help keep you out of financial and legal hot water. With that in mind, pay close attention to any changes requested by a service provider to any of the provisions contained in this section.

Also, be cognizant that there is a relationship between the *General Indemnification, Proprietary Rights Indemnification, Indemnification Procedures, Limitation of Liability*, and *Insurance* provisions contained in this section. While an indemnity (both general and for proprietary rights) can serve as a substantial risk mitigation tool for buyers, its usefulness can be eroded by a limitation of liability provision and (lack of) insurance. For example, if a limitation of liability provision (which caps a party's financial obligations for damages) is structured such that the obligation of indemnification (which requires a party to be financially liable to the other party) is substantially limited, a buyer may have no real protection because the seller has a limited dollar amount for which it's responsible. Further, even if an indemnification provision is not substantially limited by the limitation of liability provision, a seller may be "judgment-proof" if it has insufficient insurance or no insurance. In other words, if a seller has no insurance or has no substantial assets to draw from to pay for any financial liabilities resulting from the seller's obligation of indemnification, the obligation is meaningless. Therefore, limitation of liability and insurance provisions are critical to consider in conjunction with indemnification provisions.

If you're unsure of the impact of any changes made by a service provider to the provisions contained in this section or you don't feel comfortable negotiating the legalese of this section, it would be prudent to seek qualified legal counsel.

General Indemnification

In the context of how indemnification is commonly structured in buyer-seller contracts, it's the obligation of a contracting party (the "indemnitor") to be financially responsible ("indemnify" and "hold harmless") and legally responsible ("defend") for certain specified claims that are brought against the other contracting party (the "indemnitee") by a third-party (i.e., *not* a party to the contract). Indemnification is not considered an appropriate remedy for contract claims, such as breach of contract, between the contracting parties. With those claims, the contracting parties have other remedies available (such as liquidated damages). The indemnification commonly contained in buyer-seller contracts, such as the one in the SaaS Agreement, is referred to as a "third-party" or "contractual" indemnification. A typical third-party indemnification consists of five parts: the [1] words of promise; the [2] parties being indemnified (the "indemnitees"); the [3] scope of indemnification; the [4] subject of indemnification; and, [5] express exclusions from indemnification.

Under the *General Indemnification* provision, the service provider as the indemnitor has the [1] duty to "indemnify, defend, and hold harmless." Those terms comprise the words of promise. To "indemnify" means to be financially liable to another party, such as to pay for settlements or judgments. To "defend" means to either provide a defense for an indemnitee or to pay for an indemnitee's own defense. Some legal authorities posit that to "hold harmless" is synonymous with "indemnify" and suggest that using either by itself would be sufficient. Some argue that "hold harmless" means something more: to "indemnify" *and* "defend." Others believe that the duty to "hold harmless" has further meaning; specifically, that it limits the indemnitee's liability and effectively bars the indemnitor from seeking any sort of contribution from the indemnitee. Still others contend that "hold harmless" has both a retrospective and prospective application, protecting against the possibility of risk of loss as well as actual loss. While it can be argued that using "indemnify" and "hold harmless" could invite a court to differentiate some meaning between the two that could prove detrimental, it's an unlikely result considering that the majority of court cases fall out with nary a difference between the two terms. When there has been a court that differentiates between the two terms, it seems that the court has already made an overall decision in the case and works to devise a differentiation to support the outcome. The best option—at least in the context of a buyer-seller contract—is to let the legal authorities quibble over the splitting of hairs and to include all three terms.

The [2] parties to be indemnified (indemnitees) are relatively straightforward: your company, as the subscriber, as well as your officers, directors, agents, and employees. You may want to name additional parties if your needs require, such as including subsidiaries, affiliated entities, and suppliers. As you would expect, the more that you include as indemnified parties, the more the service provider won't like it because expanding the parties to be indemnified expands the breadth of the service provider's risk.

The [3] scope of the indemnification describes what the indemnitor is going to be liable for—and when. For the indemnitee, the goal is to make the scope as broad as possible. In the *General Indemnification* provision, that's the case: "any and all" sorts of liabilities are included, along with attorneys' fees, costs, and expenses. That element of scope is easy to enumerate. The other element of scope—the "when"—is frequently overlooked or made ambiguous by the contract language. The duty to indemnify is, according to some definitions, not triggered until *after* there is a judgment entered against the indemnitee or a settlement agreed-upon. The duty to defend, on the other hand, is triggered as soon as a claim is made against the indemnitee. Because the indemnification scope includes "any and all" liabilities, which would include liabilities beyond a court judgment, the words "suffered by, incurred by, accrued against, charged to, or recoverable from" in the *General Indemnification* provision are used to avoid any confusion with the timing between "indemnify" and "defend." The words "suffered by" in the *General Indemnification* provision implies that you've actually had some sort of judgment or final liability charged against you and you paid it. In that case, under a duty of indemnity and barring any other facts that would waive that duty, the indemnitor is clearly going to be on the hook to reimburse you. What happens between being hit with a claim and the final judgment? Sure, there's the indemnitor's duty to provide a defense, but what does that really mean in terms of costs that you as the indemnitee might incur in that in-between timeframe? For example, when you are hit with some sort of claim, you're likely to start incurring costs right way, such as putting a legal hold in place where you have staff running around to preserve records. What happens if you do get a final judgment awarded against you for a trillion dollars? Do you have to pay it and then be reimbursed by the indemnitor? Wouldn't it be better to have the indemnitor give you the trillion dollars first or pay the trillion dollars on your behalf? To avoid any ambiguity as to when the indemnitor is responsible to reimburse you or to pay another party on your behalf, the words "incurred by, accrued against, charged to, or recoverable from" in the *General Indemnification* provision are critical because they imply you haven't necessarily paid some sort of judgment or final liability but that you do have some sort of interim actual or final prospective liability. Because a service provider doesn't want to pay up at all, or at least not until it absolutely must, some service providers will replace "which may be suffered by, incurred by, accrued against, charged to, or recoverable from any Indemnitee" with something like "which is finally adjudged against any Indemnitee" or, worse, "which has been entered against an Indemnitee as a final unappealable judgment by a court of competent jurisdiction." Your answer to that is "absolutely not"—because, but for some third-party bringing a claim against you because of something the service provider allegedly did or didn't do, you wouldn't be in the pickle you are. Quite simply, the service provider needs to step up.

The [4] subject of an indemnification defines the matters which trigger the obligation of indemnification. The matters can arise from or relate to "any act, error or omission, negligence, or misconduct" of the service provider or its affiliated parties. The list in the *General Indemnification* provision is common and includes injury, death, damage to personal and real property, payments owing to subcontractors, material misrepresentations and breaches of representations and warranties, and material breaches of any covenant (i.e., promise or obligation). The list is also, as the result of broad terms such as "any representation or warranty" and "any covenant," all encompassing. As examples, the following, among many other representations, warranties, and covenants, would be triggers of the duty to indemnify: not pay subcontractors (*Subcontractors* provision); fail to maintain a sufficient information security program (*Data Privacy and Information Security* section); infringe a third-party's proprietary rights (*Representations and Warranties – By Service Provider* provision); or, fail to comply with laws (*Compliance with Laws; Subscriber Policies and Procedures* provision). A service provider may pick at the list, redlining it to be less encompassing and narrower. As usual, when you're asked to make a concession, you'll put up a fuss and see if you can get the service provider to back down. If not, the service provider "owes you one." If you do have to concede on excluding some items from the list, don't worry, you have an ace in your pocket unless the service provider reads the language of the provision closely: the words "including, without limitation" precede the list. In other words, the enumerated list that follows isn't a limiting list (as the service provider commonly sees in other indemnification provisions, but not this one); it's merely an illustrative and incomplete list of examples. In many other indemnification provisions that the service provider routinely reviews, the subject of the indemnification, i.e., the list of triggers, is typically a finite list. Thus, the service provider's attention is focused on the list, whittling it down, and not necessarily on the few seemingly unimportant words preceding the list. If the service provider doesn't catch this nuance, it's on the hook to indemnify you against pretty much everything.

Nearly universal in every indemnification provision is one or more [5] express exclusions from the duty of indemnification. Here, the *General Indemnification* provision includes the common exclusion that the duty to indemnify doesn't apply to any claim that resulted from the acts or omissions of the party seeking indemnification. In other words, the service provider isn't responsible to indemnify you if you're the one that caused the claim to occur.

Sellers—particularly attorneys that represent them—don't like third-party indemnification when they're the indemnitor because it means they could be financially and legally liable. On the other hand, those same sellers (and their attorneys) really like it when the buyer (you) is the indemnitor. When a seller is the intended indemnitor, it will often attempt to shift the financial and legal risk of third-party liability to the buyer even when the seller is a fault—that shift of risk is accomplished by diluting the indemnification provision; for example, by limiting the words of promise, the indemnitees, the scope, and the subject. A telltale sign of a seller's love-hate relationship with third-party indemnification is when you see two indemnification provisions in the seller's contract template: one for the seller and one for you. You can imagine which one of those provisions isn't going to be favorable to you (hint: both).

Under a buyer-seller contract, the buyer commonly seeks a unilateral general indemnification provision (where only the seller is the indemnifying party) on the basis that the buyer is the party most likely to have a significant third-party claim asserted against it as a result of the contract and as a result of the seller's performance (or lack thereof). On the other hand, the seller is not likely to have a third-party claim asserted against it as a result of the buyer's performance (or lack thereof) because, arguably, a buyer's only substantial performance obligation to the seller under a buyer-seller contract is payment. Considering that, you should start contract negotiations with a unilateral indemnification provision in your SaaS Agreement but it's more likely than not a service provider will ask for mutuality. If you do have to concede to a mutual indemnification, don't be too worried that all of the foregoing discussion of how broad and all-encompassing the *General Indemnification* provision is will come back to haunt you because you're now subject to the same provision. The reason to not worry, is because, realistically, the likelihood of your being a cause of a third-party claim against the service provider is very low (assuming you're being reasonable and prudent in the performance of your obligations under the SaaS Agreement).

15.1 <u>General Indemnification</u>. Service Provider agrees to [1]indemnify, defend, and hold harmless [2]Subscriber and its officers, directors, agents, and employees (each, an "Indemnitee") from and against [3]any and all liabilities, damages, losses, expenses, claims, demands, suits, fines, or judgments (each, a "Claim," and collectively, the "Claims"), including reasonable attorneys' fees, costs, and expenses incidental thereto, which may be suffered by, incurred by, accrued against, charged to, or recoverable from any Indemnitee, [4]by reason of any Claim arising out of or relating to any act, error or omission, negligence, or misconduct of Service Provider, its officers, directors, agents, employees, and subcontractors, during the performance of this Agreement, including, without limitation, Claims arising out of or relating to: (a) bodily injury (including death) or damage to tangible personal or real property; (b) any payment required to be paid to subcontractors, if any, of Service Provider; (c) any material misrepresentation or breach of warranty of any representation or warranty set forth in this Agreement; or, (d) any material breach of any covenant set forth in this Agreement; [5]<u>provided, however</u>, that the foregoing indemnity shall not apply to the extent that the applicable Claim resulted from the acts or omissions of an Indemnitee.

Proprietary Rights Indemnification

Under the *Representations and Warranties – By Service Provider* provision, the service provider represents and warrants that it had all necessary rights to provide the services to you and that the services performed by the service provider won't infringe anyone's intellectual property rights. What happens if the service provider doesn't have the necessary rights or does infringe? Similar to the *General Indemnification* provision, the *Proprietary Rights Indemnification* provision imposes a duty on the service provider to indemnify, defend, and hold you harmless where it violates a third-party's proprietary rights. You'd be correct in thinking that such a violation could be covered by the *General Indemnification* provision where indemnification is triggered by "any material misrepresentation or breach of warranty of any representation or warranty set forth in this Agreement." Even though the *Proprietary Rights Indemnification* and *General Indemnification* provisions are alike, the reason for a completely separate provision is because of the unique remedies that go beyond paying and defending.

As with the *General Indemnification* provision, this provision uses the [1] same words of promise, [2] same parties to be indemnified, and [3] same scope. The [4] subject is infringement or misappropriation of any proprietary right throughout the world. [5] If the service provider gets slapped with an injunction and can no longer provide you with the services, it not only needs to indemnify you and provide you with a defense, it must [6] try to work with the party that has been infringed and negotiate the right for you to continue using the services, or, if it can't do that, [7] replace or modify the services so that the service provider is no longer infringing on someone else's proprietary rights. [8] If the service provider is unable to do either one [6, 7] of the foregoing or determines that it's "commercially unreasonable," then it has to [8] return any amounts that you've prepaid and provide the services described in the *Transition Services* provision without charge (should there be any charge).

A service provider may take issue with [4] the subject of indemnification similar to the issues that a service provider will have relating to the applicable representations and warranties under the *Representations and Warranties – By Service Provider* provision; specifically, to limit the scope of proprietary rights to the U.S.

Unlike the express exclusion from indemnification contained in the *General Indemnification* provision, the *Proprietary Rights Indemnification* doesn't contain any such exclusion. A service provider may, however, want to limit [4] the subject of indemnification by including one or more express exclusions that are specific to proprietary rights. If so, such exclusions could include something to the effect of the following, which is generally reasonable and acceptable:

> "...provided, however, that Service Provider shall have no such obligation of indemnification where the Claim results from: (a) Services based on specifications or direction provided by Subscriber; (b) Subscriber's use of the Services in a manner other than which was intended under this Agreement; (c) modifications to the Services made by anyone other than Service Provider who has not been authorized by Service Provider; (d) Subscriber's unauthorized alteration, modification, or revision of the Services; or, (e) Subscriber's combination of the Services with other services or materials in a manner that is not recommended or anticipated by Service Provider."

15.2   Proprietary Rights Indemnification. Service Provider agrees to [1]indemnify, defend, and hold harmless [2]Indemnitees from and against [3]any and all Claims, including reasonable attorneys' fees, costs, and expenses incidental thereto, which may be suffered by, incurred by, accrued against, charged to, or recoverable from any Indemnitee, [4]by reason of any Claim arising out of or relating to the Services infringing or misappropriating any United States or foreign patent, copyright, trade secret, trademark, or other proprietary right. [5]In the event that Service Provider is enjoined from providing the Services and such injunction is not dissolved within thirty (30) calendar days, or in the event that Subscriber is adjudged, in any final order of a court of competent jurisdiction from which no appeal is taken, to have infringed upon or misappropriated any patent, copyright, trade secret, trademark, or other proprietary right in the access or use of the Services, then Service Provider shall, at its expense: [6](a) obtain for Subscriber the right to continue using such Services; [7](b) replace or modify such Services so that they do not infringe upon or misappropriate such proprietary right and is free to be used by Subscriber; or, [8](c) in the event that Service Provider is unable or determines, in its reasonable judgment, that it is commercially unreasonable to do either of the aforementioned, Service Provider shall reimburse to Subscriber any prepaid fees and the full cost associated with any Transition Services.

Indemnification Procedures

As previously explained, both the *General Indemnification* and *Proprietary Rights Indemnification* provisions impose a duty to defend on the service provider. In the event of a claim, and rather than figuring out what to do in the heat of the moment, the *Indemnification Procedures* provision provides clarity and certainty by describing the procedures both parties are to follow when seeking indemnification.

The moment you're [1] threatened with a claim by a third-party, become aware that you will have a claim made against you, or discover that a claim has been filed against you, you need to immediately give notice to the service provider. It's important for the service provider to get out in front of any claim so as to mitigate any further liabilities and to do whatever it needs to do administratively to prepare (such as give notice to its insurer, which likely won't cover a claim if it didn't get prompt notice). [2] If you're not prompt or fail to give notice, that's not an excuse for the service provider to get out of defending and indemnifying you—unless your delay did actually jeopardize the service provider's ability to defend you. For example, if you had notice of a claim, had a default judgment entered against you because you failed to respond, and then you seek reimbursement from the service provider, the service provider isn't required to indemnify you because your delay impacted the service provider's ability to negotiate a settlement or defend against the claim in such a way that damages were avoided, weren't awarded, or were minimized.

The service provider has [3] control of the defense and settlement negotiations and you're not permitted to defend against or respond to a claim. However, [4] if you determine that the service provider isn't defending you diligently and you're going to have a default judgment awarded against you, you do have the right to your own defense. Of anything a service provider will take issue with in this provision, it will be its obligation for your expenses should you decided to independently defend. However, the reason for the service provider being on the hook is one of motivation: for the service provider to provide a robust defense, and, if it doesn't, to reimburse you for your providing that defense. In any case, [5] you have the right to monitor the service provider's defense of you albeit at your expense.

Of course, you're required to [6] cooperate with the service provider in providing you with a defense. For purposes of this provision, "cooperate" means to, for example, provide documents, information and responses, to be available to assist the service provider, help strategize, and to attend depositions. [7] Should your cooperation result in any costs to you, including attorneys' fees, the service provider's obligation of indemnification kicks in and it has to reimburse you.

15.3   Indemnification Procedures.   [1]Promptly after receipt by Subscriber of a threat, notice, or filing of any Claim against an Indemnitee, Subscriber shall give notice thereof to Service Provider, [2]provided that failure to give or delay in giving such notice shall not relieve Service Provider of any liability it may have to the Indemnitee except to the extent that Service Provider demonstrates that the defense of the Claim is prejudiced thereby. [3]Service Provider shall have sole control of the defense and of all negotiations for settlement of a Claim and Subscriber shall not independently defend or respond to a Claim; provided, however, that: [4](a) Subscriber may defend or respond to a Claim, at Service Provider's expense, if Subscriber's counsel determines, in its sole discretion, that such defense or response is necessary to preclude a default judgment from being entered against an Indemnitee; and, [5](b) Subscriber shall have the right, at its own expense, to monitor Service Provider's defense of a Claim. At Service Provider's request, [6]Subscriber shall reasonably cooperate with Service Provider in defending against or settling a Claim; provided, however, that [7]Service Provider shall reimburse Subscriber for all reasonable out-of-pocket costs incurred by Subscriber (including, without limitation, reasonable attorneys' fees and expenses) in providing such cooperation.

Third-Party Beneficiaries

While the *Third-Party Beneficiaries* provision is normally boilerplate found near the end of contract with all of the other boilerplate (that most people don't take a close look at), the provision is included in the *Indemnification; Liability; Insurance* section in the SaaS Agreement because, [1] for purposes of indemnification, parties other than you, as the subscriber, are clearly beneficiaries to the SaaS Agreement. This provision provides for that but then [2] goes on to include the typical "no beneficiary" language, i.e., that persons or entities that are not signatories to the SaaS Agreement or that are not indemnified parties have no rights or authority. If the *General Indemnification* provision is made mutual, the first and second sentence of this provision must be similarly modified.

15.4   Third-Party Beneficiaries. [1]For the purposes of this Section and Service Provider's obligations hereunder, non-party Indemnitees are third-party beneficiaries of this Agreement in accordance with its terms. Any action or consent taken by Subscriber on its own behalf is binding upon the non-party

Indemnitees for the purposes of this Section. [2]Other than as provided for in this Section, this Agreement is for the sole benefit of the signatories hereto and their permitted successors and assigns. Nothing, express or implied, in this Agreement is intended to create or be construed to create any rights of enforcement in any persons or entities who are neither signatories to this Agreement nor non-party Indemnitees.

Limitation of Liability

Other than an indemnification provision, a limitation of liability provision is perhaps the most important risk-shifting provision in a buyer-seller contract because it shields (limits) or exposes (doesn't limit) a party to financial liability for damages that arise under the contract. The limit described in a limitation of liability provision constitutes the maximum financial liability for damages recoverable by one party against the other party. Properly drafted, the provision can provide protection against significant liability (for the party that has to pay up) and too little liability (for the party that has been damaged). Capitalized text is commonly used to ensure that the provision is conspicuous and to avoid any argument that the limitation was hidden by embodying it among less critical provisions.

The *Limitation of Liability* provision is comprised of four parts. The four parts are common to this type of provision but might be found in different order from contract to contract. The [1] first part is typically referred to as the "exculpation" from the limitation of liability. When a contract is breached, the recognized remedy for the non-breaching party is the recovery of damages that result *directly* from the breach. Consequential damages (also sometimes referred to as special or indirect damages) are those damages that don't directly result from a breach but are an indirect consequence of the breach (such as lost profits). Because consequential damages in many cases are not reasonably foreseeable, parties typically agree—as is the case in this provision—that no party will be liable for these types of damages.

The [2] second part contains an "exclusion" to the foregoing exculpation. Under this exclusion, a party *will* be liable for consequential damages where the party caused the damage through its gross negligence and willful misconduct. There are varying degrees of possible misconduct that range along a continuum, from ordinary negligence to gross negligence to willful misconduct. Ordinary negligence involves the failure to exercise a standard of care that a reasonably prudent and careful person would have exercised in a similar situation. Gross negligence involves the conscious and voluntary disregard of the need to use reasonable care. Willful misconduct is the wanton and reckless disregard of a standard of care. Another way to think about the differences is that ordinary negligence is "should have known better," gross negligence is "sort of knew better but did it anyway," and willful misconduct is "absolutely knew better and, regardless, did it intentionally and on purpose." Thus, you'll get consequential damages if the service provider voluntarily or intentionally violates its duty of care to you.

The [3] third part is the actual limitation of liability, which is the core of the provision. This part of the provision states that a party is liable for direct damages up to the stated limitation. The limitation can be specified quantitatively by stating an exact dollar amount (such as one million dollars) or can be described qualitatively such as "fees paid or payable under the Agreement." When described qualitatively, sellers such as service providers frequently prefer "fees paid" and will try to exclude "payable." In fact, most contract templates originated by sellers will include only "fees paid." This makes little sense considering that there will likely be a lag between when a contract is made effective and when the seller is first paid and, in that timeframe, the buyer would have no protection because the seller's liability is limited to $0 (because no fees were yet paid). The language of this provision is qualitative, and, in your case, the fees you have paid or will pay may be insufficient (too low of a limit). Therefore, you may need to state an actual dollar amount.

The [4] fourth part is typically called an "exception" to the limitation of liability. An exception means that, for the stated exception, there is no limitation of liability and a party's liability relating to the exception will be unlimited. Commonly, a party's obligation of indemnification, damages caused by a party's negligence (usually gross) or willful misconduct, or a breach of a party's obligation of confidentiality are exceptions to the limit and, therefore, there is no limitation with respect to the exceptions. The exception relating to a party's obligation of indemnification is critical, particularly considering infringement. Should a service provider allegedly infringe a third-party's proprietary rights—which seems to be more and more of a likely occurrence due to the rise of so-called "patent trolls"—and the third-party brings some sort of claim against you, the costs associated with defending against the claim and the costs of your remedies (described in the *Proprietary Rights Indemnification* provision) could be enormous. If the limitation of liability is contractually capped and the cap is subsequently reached, a service provider has no further obligation to assist you. Thus, particularly as it relates to the indemnification exception to the limitation of liability, you'll have to bargain hard if the service provider pushes back on the exception.

In some cases, where the parties have unequal negotiation leverage or one party is more sophisticated than the other, the limitation of liability may be unilateral—meaning that one party has limited liability and the other party has unlimited liability. With service providers, the negotiation leverage is clearly unequal (a subscriber *or* a service provider may have the negotiating advantage based on the situation) but it's more efficient to start with a mutual limitation of liability since both parties are generally sophisticated (especially after reading this book). If a service provider's legal representative gets involved in the negotiation of the SaaS Agreement, that individual will likely have some sort of "input" relating to the *Limitation of Liability* provision. That input will inevitably entail a lower limit for the service provider and / or a higher limit for you as the subscriber (as the liable party). Read and consider all requested changes carefully.

15.5   Limitation of Liability.   NOTWITHSTANDING ANY OTHER PROVISION SET FORTH HEREIN, [1]NEITHER PARTY SHALL BE LIABLE FOR ANY INDIRECT, SPECIAL, AND / OR CONSEQUENTIAL DAMAGES ARISING OUT OF OR IN

CONNECTION WITH THIS AGREEMENT; PROVIDED, HOWEVER, THAT [2]THE FOREGOING EXCULPATION OF LIABILITY SHALL NOT APPLY WITH RESPECT TO DAMAGES INCURRED AS A RESULT OF THE GROSS NEGLIGENCE OR WILLFUL MISCONDUCT OF A PARTY. [3]A PARTY SHALL BE LIABLE TO THE OTHER FOR ANY DIRECT DAMAGES ARISING OUT OF OR RELATING TO ITS PERFORMANCE OR FAILURE TO PERFORM UNDER THIS AGREEMENT; PROVIDED, HOWEVER, THAT THE LIABILITY OF A PARTY, WHETHER BASED ON AN ACTION OR CLAIM IN CONTRACT, EQUITY, NEGLIGENCE, TORT, OR OTHERWISE FOR ALL EVENTS, ACTS, OR OMISSIONS UNDER THIS AGREEMENT SHALL NOT EXCEED THE FEES PAID OR PAYABLE UNDER THIS AGREEMENT, AND PROVIDED, FURTHER, THAT THE [4]FOREGOING LIMITATION SHALL NOT APPLY TO: (A) A PARTY'S OBLIGATIONS OF INDEMNIFICATION, AS FURTHER DESCRIBED IN THIS AGREEMENT; (B) DAMAGES CAUSED BY A PARTY'S GROSS NEGLIGENCE OR WILLFUL MISCONDUCT; OR, (C) A PARTY'S BREACH OF ITS OBLIGATIONS OF CONFIDENTIALITY, AS FURTHER DESCRIBED IN THIS AGREEMENT. This Section shall survive the termination of this Agreement.

Insurance

Where a party to a contract causes some sort of damage or injury to the other party, the party at fault will generally be responsible for such damage or injury subject to the terms and conditions of the contract. While some service providers may be well capitalized, others won't have sufficient liquid assets or, for that matter, any assets at all, to cover potential liabilities that arise from a contract. Considering the possibility that something might go awry, it would be prudent for a service provider to have insurance to cover any potential liabilities. Otherwise, without insurance, good luck collecting on any claim or judgment you might be awarded against your service provider.

A service provider isn't likely to take any significant issue with the *Insurance* provision, as the language is common to most buyer-seller contracts. If a service provider wants to tweak the language a bit, that's probably fine, but be sure to examine any changes—such as coverage limitations—carefully. If a service provider makes any substantive changes, doing so should raise a big, red flag and you need to question why the service provider isn't willing to provide the required insurance coverage.

The [1] service provider, at its expense, must provide the types and amounts (per occurrence and / or in total) of coverage specified in the *Insurance* provision by qualified insurance carriers. [2] Commercial general liability insurance (frequently called "CGL" insurance) covers claims made against you, the subscriber, as a result of the services performed under the SaaS Agreement and will pay for the defense the service provider has an obligation to provide you under its duty of indemnification. CGL insurance coverage provides protection against bodily injury and property damage claims arising from the operations of the service provider and applies to its contractual liability (which covers torts). A CGL insurance policy normally limits all loss payments to two aggregate limits, one for products / services and completed operations and one for all other losses.

Excess liability insurance provides additional protection when the service provider exceeds insurance limits on underlying insurance policies. Excess liability insurance is generally the most affordable way to get higher policy limits on other insurance policies (rather than having higher limits on each of the other insurance policies). However, excess liability insurance doesn't extend coverage on a professional liability insurance policy. Excess liability insurance is sometimes referred to as "umbrella insurance," but there is a difference between the two. Excess liability goes into effect only when the underlying policies are totally exhausted, while umbrella insurance covers claims in excess of limits *and* can also fill coverage gaps in underlying policies. Therefore, an umbrella policy can become the primary policy for certain claims.

If the service provider has employees, which is likely, workers' compensation coverage is mandatory and employers' liability, which is not mandatory, is an absolute must. Worker's compensation insurance protects employees by paying an employee's medical bills for work-related injuries and illnesses and employers' liability insurance protects the employer by paying the employer if the injured or sickened employee sues the employer. The two forms of insurance are usually included in the same policy.

Generally, professional liability insurance provides coverage for actual or alleged errors, omissions, negligence, breach of duty, misleading statements, and similar claims resulting from the performance—or non-performance—of professional services. Most policies cover both the defense costs (e.g., attorneys' fees, court costs) and settlements or judgments. Intentional wrongdoing is typically not covered. Professional liability insurance is required by law in some areas for certain kinds of professional practices (especially medical and legal) but is also frequently required by buyers under buyer-seller contracts, such as the SaaS Agreement, where the buyer is a beneficiary of the advice or service provided by the seller. While traditionally for professionals such as physicians and attorneys, professional liability insurance can be specifically purchased for IT professionals and IT services. This emerging type of professional liability insurance is referred to as "technology errors and omissions insurance," "IT liability insurance," or "technology professional liability insurance."

It's required that the [3] service provider name you as an additional insured under its policies. An additional insured is a person or party other than the named insured listed on an insurance policy who is protected under the terms of the policy. An additional insured doesn't own the policy but is added by endorsement or is referred to in the definition of "insured" in the policy itself. As an additional insured, you enjoy the benefit of insurance protection from the service provider's policy but keep in mind that you likely don't have control over the defense of any claim—insurers are usually provided with the exclusive right to control the defense of claims that they cover. Since it's possible that an additional insured might bring a claim against another additional insured under the same policy of insurance, the service provider is required to provide coverage that includes a cross liability clause. This type of clause is usually standard in CGL insurance policies and ensures that claims by one insured against another are treated as if separate policies had been issued to each insured.

[4] Because commercial general liability policies are primarily designed to cover claims directly against an insured, such policies sometimes exclude liabilities transferred by way of contract—such as tort liability related to third-party bodily injury or property damage. If your service provider's CGL insurance had such an exclusion, the *General Indemnification* provision, which includes indemnification for bodily injury death, and damage to personal or real property, would be essentially eviscerated. To avoid this problem, a service provider is specifically required to have contractual liability coverage as a part of its CGL insurance.

The *Insurance* provision requires the coverage to be [5] "primary without right of contribution." You want the service provider's insurance to be the first ("primary") to respond to any claim. You don't want your insurance to be required to contribute first with the service provider's insurance covering any excess. This requirement helps to keep the cost of your insurance coverage lower.

Not that the service provider is going to pull a fast one on you, but the [6] insurance is only good as long it's in effect, covers what you need it to cover, and provides coverage to the required limit. To ensure that you still have the specified coverage, should there be any cancellations or material changes to the insurance policies required by the SaaS Agreement, the service provider must notify you within the specified period. During that notice period, you'll have plenty of time to force the service provider to make any corrections to insurance coverage. Also, [7] if your exposure to the service provider increases because, for example, you increase the scope of services, you have the right request an increase in the coverage for CGL insurance and professional liability insurance.

To make certain that the service provider does indeed have the right types and amounts of insurance, [8] the service provider has the obligation to provide certificates of insurance for your records. A certificate of insurance or "COI" is generally issued by or on behalf of the insurance carrier only as a matter of information—a COI doesn't confers any actual rights upon the certificate holder that have not already been provided in the actual insurance policy. A COI merely provides evidence that certain insurance policies are in place on the date the COI is issued, and that these policies have the limits and policy periods shown. The service provider is also required to provide you with a COI in advance of any renewals or substitutions of coverage. Similar to the earlier clause relating to cancellations or material changes, the service provider must notify you in advance, which allows you time to address any concerns you have with any renewal or substitution.

15.6   Insurance.   [1]Service Provider shall, at its own expense, procure and maintain in full force and effect during the term of this Agreement, policies of insurance, of the types and in the minimum amounts as follows, with responsible insurance carriers duly qualified in those states (locations) where the Services are to be performed, covering the operations of Service Provider, pursuant to this Agreement: [2]commercial general liability ($1,000,000 per occurrence, $2,000,000 aggregate); excess liability ($2,000,000 per occurrence, $2,000,000 aggregate); workers' compensation (statutory limits) and employers' liability ($500,000 per accident); and, professional liability ($1,000,000 per occurrence, $1,000,000 aggregate). Subscriber shall be [3]named as an additional insured in such policies which shall contain standard cross liability clauses. Service Provider shall cause the [4]liability it assumed under this Agreement to be specifically insured under the contractual liability section of the liability insurance policies. The liability policy shall be [5]primary without right of contribution from any insurance by Subscriber. Such policies shall require that Subscriber be given [6]no less than thirty (30) calendar days prior written notice of any cancellation thereof or material change therein. Subscriber shall have the right to [7]request an adjustment of the limits of liability for commercial general liability and professional liability insurance as Service Provider's exposure to Subscriber increases. [8]Service Provider shall provide Subscriber with certificates of insurance evidencing all of the above coverage, including all special requirements specifically noted above, and shall provide Subscriber with certificates of insurance evidencing renewal or substitution of such insurance thirty (30) calendar days prior to the effective date of such renewal or substitution.

General

Like many other contracts, the SaaS Agreement contains a section of boilerplate contract provisions. While some of the boilerplate provisions in the SaaS Agreement are relatively straightforward and don't require explanation, there are certain boilerplate provisions, described below, that are worth examining more closely.

Relationship between Subscriber and Service Provider

It's typical in buyer-seller contracts to include a provision that describes the relationship between the parties. The primary reasons for the provision is to avoid agency-related problems such as where one party appears to have (but doesn't have) authority to bind the other party and employer-employee problems such as co-employment. Co-employment is a legal doctrine that applies when two legally distinct employers have an employer-employee relationship with the same person. If that occurs, a seller's employee may be deemed to be an employee of the buyer for legal purposes such as employee benefits or taxes. To avoid such problems, this *Relationship between Subscriber and Service Provider* provision [1] states that the parties are completely independent and that the service provider doesn't have the authority to bind you in any way. In addition, the provision makes it clear that the [2] service provider doesn't hold any special relationship with you. If the service provider does attempt to bind you or does act, for example, as an unauthorized agent, the service provider—and not you—will be liable for any damages.

16.1   <u>Relationship between Subscriber and Service Provider</u>. Service Provider represents and warrants that [1]it is an independent contractor with no authority to contract for Subscriber or in any way to bind or to commit Subscriber to any agreement of any kind or to assume any liabilities of any nature in the name of or on behalf of Subscriber. [2]Under no circumstances shall Service Provider, or any of its staff, if any, hold itself out as or be considered an agent employee, joint venture, or partner of Subscriber. In recognition of Service Provider's status as an independent contractor, Subscriber shall carry no Workers' Compensation insurance or any health or accident insurance to cover Service Provider or Service Provider's agents or staff, if any. Subscriber shall not pay any contributions to Social Security, unemployment insurance, federal or state withholding taxes, any other applicable taxes whether federal, state, or local, nor provide any other contributions or benefits which might be expected in an employer-employee relationship. Neither Service Provider nor its staff, if any, shall be eligible for, participate in, or accrue any direct or indirect benefit under any other compensation, benefit, or pension plan of Subscriber.

Governing Law

This provision—also called a "choice of law" provision—specifies the body of law of a particular state or jurisdiction that governs the rights and responsibilities of parties under the SaaS Agreement. Strategically, you should prefer that the governing law of the SaaS Agreement be the law of the jurisdiction in which you're located because the cost to litigate a contract dispute in a service provider's distant jurisdiction is inherently higher and because the other jurisdiction may be potentially hostile to your claim or defense. Within limits, parties may choose which jurisdiction's law will govern matters related to contract formation, interpretation, and enforceability. A governing law provision usually includes, as is the case with the SaaS Agreement, both the substantive law to apply to a contract as well as the procedural law. It's possible, but not common, to have one jurisdiction's law govern a contract and another jurisdiction serve as the place (forum / venue) where the substantive law is applied. For example, contracting parties could agree that Georgia law applies but that Florida will be the forum state. In this example, the Florida courts would apply Georgia law. Mostly, a court will apply whatever governing law was selected by contracting parties provided that the governing law does not conflict with the public policy of the forum state. However, if the selected governing law is different from the state of domicile for the contracting parties, a court in the forum state generally requires some sort of nexus between the selected governing law, the forum, and the contracting parties.

For the same reason that you want your state law to govern the SaaS Agreement, a service provider will want its state law to apply, particularly considering that it's more likely for the service provider to be sued under the SaaS Agreement than you (because the service provider is doing more "performing" under the SaaS Agreement and has more exposure to something going wrong). In cases where neither party will budge on their own jurisdiction's governing law, as a compromise, parties often agree to either New York or Illinois law to govern the contract. New York is a common compromise because of New York City's position as one of the world's major financial and commercial centers—meaning that New York has well-established and balanced civil and case law as it relates to business transactions and contract matters. The same goes for Chicago, thus Illinois also makes sense as a governing law compromise.

16.2   <u>Governing Law</u>. This Agreement shall be governed by and construed in accordance with the laws of the [State Name] and the federal laws of the United States of America. Service Provider hereby consents and submits to the jurisdiction and forum of the state and federal courts in the [State Name] in all questions and controversies arising out of this Agreement.

Attorneys' Fees and Costs

In the U.S., there's a custom that, unless authorized by statute or otherwise agreed upon in a contract, each party to a dispute pays its own attorneys' fees. This custom, called the "American Rule," means that you'll foot your own legal bill even when the service provider is at fault for materially breaching the SaaS Agreement and you had to file suit to get the service provider to make good. There are other very narrow exceptions to the American Rule, such as bad faith, which eviscerate the rule but that's not important for discussion here—which is how to contract around the American Rule.

The rationale for the American Rule is that potential plaintiffs would arguably be discouraged from seeking legal recourse knowing that they would have to pick up attorneys' fees for the other party (the defendant) if the plaintiff lost. So why call it the "American Rule?" Well, it's uniquely American. In contrast to the American Rule, the "English Rule" in the United Kingdom and rules in many other countries award attorneys' fees and costs to the prevailing party. The rationale for the English Rule and similar rules is exactly opposite of the American Rule: a litigant (whether bringing a claim or defending a claim) is entitled to legal representation and, if successful, should not be out of pocket by reason of the litigant's own legal fees. Parties to a contract who don't want the American Rule to apply can bind themselves (contractually) to the English Rule by writing into their contract a provision awarding attorneys' fees to the prevailing party, payable by the losing party. These provisions are often referred to as "fee shifting" or "attorneys' fees" provisions.

In the context of a buyer-seller contract, and from a buyer's perspective, the question is whether to include an attorneys' fees provision. Generally, under a buyer-seller contract, it's more likely that the seller will be the subject of a claim or lawsuit (meaning, as either the respondent or defendant) versus the buyer. The reasoning is that a seller has numerous obligations of performance under a buyer-seller contract and a buyer has a limited number (the main obligation being to pay the seller). Thus, more often than not, it makes sense to include an attorneys' fees provision because the seller will more likely be on the "sharp end" of a lawsuit. To that end, the *Attorneys' Fees and Costs* provision is included in the SaaS Agreement and [1] applies to any sort of legal proceeding. In addition to attorneys' fees, the provision [2] encompasses other associated costs and expenses such as court costs, fees for filing documents with the court, payments for court reporters, fees for expert witnesses, as well as costs of photocopying, printing, postage, telephone, messenger services, travel, and so on. The provision is mutual, which means you'll be on the hook for paying attorneys' fees if you don't prevail on either a claim brought by you or by the service provider.

Some jurisdictions have legislated exceptions to the American Rule, so you may want to check your jurisdiction. However, checking whether your jurisdiction has an exception or not is made moot by virtue of including the *Attorneys' Fees and Costs* provision in the SaaS Agreement.

16.3   <u>Attorneys' Fees and Costs</u>. In [1]any arbitration, litigation, or other proceeding, informal or formal, by which one party either seeks to enforce this Agreement or seeks a declaration of any rights or obligations under this Agreement, the non-prevailing party shall pay the prevailing party's [2]costs and expenses, including but not limited to, reasonable attorneys' fees.

Compliance with Laws; Subscriber Policies and Procedures

A provision that requires the parties to a contract to comply with all laws and regulations is fairly common (as is the warranty of compliance with laws contained in the *Representations and Warranties – Mutual* provision). Because of the nature of their business, for example, housing PII for subscribers, service providers are subject to many different laws and regulations. You, as the subscriber, may have certain compliance obligations as well. Therefore, it makes sense to have an express affirmation in the SaaS Agreement that [1] the parties will comply accordingly with all applicable laws and regulations. The provision goes a bit further in that it [2] requires the service provider to comply with *your* policies and procedures. For example, you may have certain requirements related to data handling that you want the service provider to abide by. If you don't have any such requirements, this language should be removed. A service provider may take issue with this language and will want to know specifically what policies or procures it will be required to comply with (and the service provider will likely want to see them in advance of executing the SaaS Agreement).

16.4   <u>Compliance with Laws; Subscriber Policies and Procedures</u>. [1]Both parties agree to comply with all applicable federal, state, and local laws, executive orders and regulations issued, where applicable.   [2]Service Provider shall comply with Subscriber policies and procedures where the same are posted, conveyed, or otherwise made available to Service Provider.

Cooperation

It goes without saying that cooperation between the parties to a contract is necessary for both parties to get the benefit of the bargain. Unfortunately, it's not always intuitive in the moment, so the *Cooperation* provision helps to make clear that [1] both parties must be diligent in cooperating with each other and not do counter-productive things like unnecessarily delay or withhold performance. Further, [2] the service provider must cooperate with, and not interfere with, *any* supplier of yours such as the successor service provider, a third-party auditor, the third-party you hire to conduct a billing review as permitted by the *Billing Reviews by Third-Parties* provision, or the third-party you hire to perform escrow verification services as permitted by the *Escrow Agreement* provision. A service provider might not like being contractually obligated to cooperate and object to the provision. That'll be your opportunity to educate the service provider that there are implied covenants of good faith and fair dealing in every contract and this provision is just an express manifestation of one aspect of good faith and fair dealing. It's hard to argue with that.

16.5   Cooperation.   [1]Where agreement, approval, acceptance, consent or similar action by either party hereto is required by any provision of this Agreement, such action shall not be unreasonably delayed or withheld.   Each party will cooperate with the other by, among other things, making available, as reasonably requested by the other, management decisions, information, approvals, and acceptances in order that each party may properly accomplish its obligations and responsibilities hereunder.   [2]Service Provider will cooperate with any Subscriber supplier performing services, and all parties supplying hardware, software, communication services, and other services and products to Subscriber, including, without limitation, the Successor Service Provider.   Service Provider agrees to cooperate with such suppliers, and shall not commit or permit any act which may interfere with the performance of services by any such supplier.

Force Majeure; Excused Performance

The French-language term, "force majeure," literally means "greater force."   More broadly, it refers to an event that is a direct result of the elements of nature or "acts of God," as opposed to an event caused or created by humans.   A force majeure provision typically excuses a party from liability if some unforeseen event beyond the control of that party prevents it from performing its contractual obligations.   Because contracting parties frequently desire to encompass excused performance for events that are caused or created by humans (such as government legislation), force majeure-type provisions are also referred to as "excused performance" or "excuse of performance" provisions.   Whether or not a contract includes a force majeure and / or an excused performance provision, there are certain principles under contract law that may apply to a contract relating to excused performance: frustration of purpose, impossibility of performance, and impracticability of performance. Depending on the situation, one or more of these legal principles— again, even if not expressly included in a contract—may allow a party to terminate the contract or to discharge its obligated performance without liability. These legal principles are beyond the scope of this book but it's relevant to understand that these legal principles exist.

A force majeure / excused performance provision is fact-specific and questions arise in terms of timing and the impact of a force majeure event. When can a party invoke the provision? What happens if the other party refutes that an event specified in the provision impacts performance? Unfortunately, even the most well drafted force majeure / excused performance provision can't address every situation and a party must use its best business judgment in invoking the provision. Mostly, though, under a buyer-seller contract, the seller will have many duties (to perform) and the buyer will have really only one significant duty—and that's to pay the seller. Thus, in the context of a buyer-seller contract, a force majeure / excused performance provision will primarily benefit the seller and not the buyer. Consequently, it makes sense for the buyer to put tight controls around how the provision is triggered and how long the excused performance—if it's indeed excused—lasts.

[1] For the provision to be triggered, a delay must have occurred and be caused by an event [2] beyond the reasonable control of a party, [3] not due to a party's fault or negligence, and there [7] must be notice and a plan to resume performance. There are [9] certain events expressly listed in this provision that will not constitute a force majeure event in any case. Because service providers occasionally rely on subcontractors in providing the SaaS, service providers have been known to include the non-performance of subcontractors as a force majeure event. That's wholly unreasonable—a service provider must demand the same level of business continuity and service availability as does a subscriber demand of its service provider. For a service provider to merely shrug its shoulders and point to its subcontractors as a cause of failure as a means to claim force majeure is absolutely unacceptable (and service providers know that).

There are [8] certain responsibilities relating to the backup and recovery of subscriber data where performance will never be excused as a part of a force majeure event—it's imperative, even in the face of a force majeure event, that the integrity and security of your data is maintained. Provided that there is an appropriate force majeure event, the [4] excused performance only lasts as long as the force majeure event is beyond the control of a party. Once the effect of the force majeure event is within the reasonable control of a party (i.e., the hurricane has passed), the delayed party needs to start performing. Even if a force majeure event occurs, performance will not be excused if a party didn't try really hard to minimize the impact of the event. For example, if a service provider was located in an area known for hurricane activity (assume the beautiful city of St. Petersburg, Florida) and it didn't take proper business continuity measures, this provision won't be triggered because some portion of the delay was likely [2, 4] within the service provider's reasonable control, [3] amplified by negligence, and certainly [5] not mitigated by any effort that the service provider undertook (because it didn't undertake any such mitigating efforts). Another point on mitigation: normally, a force majeure event will give a service provider a "pass" on the requirement to achieve service levels, but that's [6] not so if the service provider didn't use its best efforts to mitigate any impact.

As an assurance that the service provider has its act together and is ready for a force majeure event, the [10] service provider must provide you, upon your request on an annual basis, with a copy of its then-current business continuity plan. The business continuity plan [11] must include, at a minimum, procedures on how the service provider: is going to backup the service and your data; "fail-over" to an operational environment; recover the service and your data; and, interact with its suppliers and subcontractors to get everything back up and running again. To ensure that the service provider's business continuity plan really isn't mere shelfware and can be successfully implemented, if necessary, the [12] service provider must test the plan and provide you, upon your request on an annual basis, with a copy of the test results. Depending on how mission-critical the services are, you may not even care about the service provider's business continuity plan (in which case you can delete the last paragraph from this provision).

16.6   Force Majeure; Excused Performance. Neither party shall be liable for delays or any failure to perform the Services or this Agreement due to causes beyond its [2]reasonable control. [1]Such delays include, but are not limited to, fire, explosion, flood or other natural catastrophe, governmental legislation, acts, orders, or regulation, strikes or labor difficulties, [3]to the extent not occasioned by the fault or negligence of the delayed party. [4]Any such excuse for delay shall last only as long as the event remains beyond the reasonable control of the delayed party. However, [5]the delayed party shall use its best efforts to minimize the delays caused by any such event beyond its reasonable control. [6]Where Service Provider fails to use its best efforts to minimize such delays, the delays shall be included in the determination of Service Level achievement. [7]The delayed party must notify the other party promptly upon the occurrence of any such event, or performance by the delayed party will not be considered excused pursuant to this Section, and inform the other party of its plans to resume performance. [8]A force majeure event does not excuse Service Provider from providing Services and fulfilling its responsibilities relating to the requirements of backup and recovery of Subscriber Data. [9]In no event shall any of the following constitute a force majeure event: (a) failure, inadequate performance, or unavailability of Service Provider's subcontractors, if any; or, (b) configuration changes, other changes, Viruses, or other errors or omissions introduced, or permitted to be introduced, by Service Provider that result in an outage or inability for Subscriber to access or use the Services. [10]Within thirty (30) calendar days following the Effective Date and on an annual basis thereafter until the termination of this Agreement, Service Provider shall provide its then-current business continuity plan ("Business Continuity Plan") to Subscriber upon Subscriber's request. The Business Continuity Plan shall [11]include: (a) Services and Subscriber Data backup and recovery procedures; (b) fail-over procedures; and, (c) how Service Provider will interact with its business continuity suppliers, if any. Service

Provider shall [12]test its Business Continuity Plan on an annual basis until the termination of this Agreement and shall provide the test results to Subscriber upon Subscriber's request.

Advertising and Publicity

Under a buyer-seller contract, sellers frequently seek to publicize their business relationships with high-profile buyers as means to gain more business. Mostly, a buyer is reluctant to allow a seller to do so because the buyer doesn't want to appear to be endorsing the products or services of the seller. Consequently, it's fairly typical to restrict a party's use of the other party's trademarks, service marks, logos, and other intellectual property in advertising and marketing without prior written approval. A service provider won't likely take issue with this provision except perhaps requesting the right to use your company's name on its customer lists (which is a reasonable request).

16.7   Advertising and Publicity.   Service Provider shall not refer to Subscriber directly or indirectly in any advertisement, news release, or publication without prior written approval from Subscriber.

Assignment of Agreement

Another common provision in buyer-seller contracts such as the SaaS Agreement, and one that is particularly important as it relates to SaaS, is the *Assignment of Agreement* provision. The concept is that a buyer selected the seller, and not someone else, to do business with and the buyer wants to have a say if the seller wishes to assign the contract (and its performance) to another party. When you select a service provider to provide SaaS and related services, you likely went through a fair amount of due diligence and selected the service provider, for a variety of good reasons, to the exclusion of other service providers. If a service provider is sold to another owner or a service provider wishes to assign the performance of the services to another entity, one or more of your many different reasons for selecting the service provider might be in jeopardy. Consequently, it makes sense that you provide consent to any assignment of the SaaS Agreement and that you have the ability to void the SaaS Agreement if you believe that the assignment isn't in your best interests. [1] If an assignment does occur, it's imperative that the service provider can transfer any licenses, contracts, or other rights that it has with third-parties to the assignee. Consequently, the provision requires the service provider to attest to having that ability. On the other hand, it shouldn't really matter to a service provider if you assign the SaaS Agreement to a different party—the service provider cares about being paid—so the provision [2] permits you to assign the SaaS Agreement to a succeeding company. With that said, a service provider may want—and reasonably so—to limit your right of assignment such that you can't assign the SaaS Agreement to a competitor of the service provider's, as unlikely as that might be.

16.10 Assignment of Agreement. This Agreement and the obligations of Service Provider hereunder are personal to Service Provider and its staff. Neither Service Provider nor any successor, receiver, or assignee of Service Provider shall directly or indirectly assign this Agreement or the rights or duties created by this Agreement, whether such assignment is effected in connection with a sale of Service Provider's assets or stock or through merger, an insolvency proceeding or otherwise, without the prior written consent of Subscriber. [1]In the case of an assignment by Service Provider, Service Provider represents and warrants that it has all requisite rights and power to transfer any agreements or other rights with third-parties whose software is incorporated into the Services or who are necessary for the performance and use of the Services. [2]Subscriber, at Subscriber's sole election, may assign any and all of its rights and obligations under this Agreement to any company that succeeds to substantially all of Subscriber's business.

Cumulative Remedies

While the *Cumulative Remedies* provision is really a boilerplate provision and doesn't require much explanation, it's highlighted here just to point out that some service providers like to make certain specified remedies "sole and exclusive"—which means that you can't pursue other remedies. "Cumulative" remedies means that you can simultaneously pursue all available remedies (such as contract remedies, monetary damages, and equitable relief) against the service provider for a breach. For example, if the service provider breaches its obligation of confidentiality and discloses your confidential information, you'll want to do any one or all of the following: terminate the SaaS Agreement (contract remedy), seek compensation for damage to your reputation (monetary damages), and seek an injunction to stop the disclosure (equitable relief). You certainly wouldn't want to be restricted to only one specified remedy and not have the ability to consider cumulative remedies. See the *Termination for Material and Repeated Failures* provision for another example of where you're permitted—and will want—cumulative remedies.

If the mindset of your service provider is to control breach risk and stick with "sole and exclusive" remedies, you'll hear some griping when you get to this provision. The service provider might have what sounds like a good argument to strike this provision and get you to agree to "sole and exclusive" remedies. If so, remind the service provider that it would be the one most likely to cause a breach and should be fully responsible. You just want to be made whole and that's all a court will let you get under your SaaS Agreement anyway. Also, if you're operating in a highly regulated industry (for example, involving electronic protected health information), there might be other remedies at law that apply and aren't captured in the SaaS Agreement. You don't want to forgo those remedies by agreeing to strike this provision and going with "sole and exclusive" remedies. Keep in mind, however, that some remedies—such as liquidated damages—are by their very nature, "sole and exclusive" remedies.

16.3   Cumulative Remedies. All rights and remedies of Subscriber herein shall be in addition to all other rights and remedies available at law or in equity, including, without limitation, specific performance against Service Provider for the enforcement of this Agreement, and temporary and permanent injunctive relief.

Exhibit A

As previously explained, the SaaS Agreement is comprised of two separate components: the master agreement component (the legal terms and conditions) and the exhibit component (the specific scope of the services; the business terms). The exhibit component, Exhibit A, will be unique to the SaaS you're contracting and for your unique needs, but the following sections are likely to be generally consistent from one SaaS subscription to another.

Services Description

Enter a detailed description of the services to be provided by the service provider. As appropriate, documents describing the services can be "attached hereto and incorporated herein."

Start Date and End Date

Indicate the start date and end date of the services. These dates represent the term of the services. If the services are not required until after the customization / integrations services, training services, etc. are completed, be sure to indicate that the start date for the services may be later than the start date for, for example, the customization / integration services. The reason for staggering the start date is to avoid paying for services that can't be productively used out of the box—otherwise, you'll essentially be paying for shelfware.

Authorized Users and Services Fees

Indicate the initial number of authorized users and associated rates. Additionally, describe "tiers" or numbers and corresponding rates to purchase additional authorized users. Describing such tiers and rates in advance helps to avoid pricing surprises down the road. Be clear as to the type of pricing model; for example, scalable pricing, module pricing, per seat pricing, usage-based pricing. The SaaS Agreement assumes a scalable and elastic per-user pricing model. Also, include the billing frequency, such as monthly, quarterly, or annually.

Storage Threshold(s)

Describe the initial data storage provided by the service provider and any additional "tiers" of storage.

Storage Fees

Describe storage fees, if any, for the initial data storage provided by the service provider as well as for any additional "tiers" of storage. Similar to the *Authorized Users and Services Fees* section, describe "tiers" and corresponding rates for possible future needs to ensure price predictability.

Technical Support Description

This section assumes that you will require some sort of technical support to facilitate your productive use of the services. This section is merely an example and will likely require significant modification for your specific subscription. Note that any authorized user has the ability to request technical support; some service providers will limit requestors to designated individuals of the subscriber who represent authorized users (essentially, a tier one level of support is provided by the subscriber).

Technical Support Description. Service Provider will provide to Subscriber telephone and email support ("Technical Support") twenty-four (24) hours per day, seven (7) days per week, three-hundred-sixty-five (365) days per year. Technical Support will include any research and resolution activity performed by Service Provider.

a) <u>Request for Technical Support</u>. Authorized Users will make Technical Support requests by calling or emailing Service Provider's Technical Support staff or by submitting a request via Service Provider's customer service web portal. The Technical Support staff shall assign to the request the Problem Severity Level (as defined herein) indicated by the requestor.

b) <u>Problem Severity Levels 1 and 2 Response and Resolution</u>. For Technical Support requests not made by telephone, within the Request Response Time of such a request, Service Provider shall confirm to the requestor receipt of the request by Service Provider. If a Problem Severity Level 1 or 2 request cannot be corrected to the reasonable satisfaction of the requestor within the Request Resolution Time after the requestor makes the initial request for Technical Support, Service Provider will: (a) immediately escalate the request to Service Provider's management; (b) take and continue to take the actions which will most expeditiously resolve the request; (c) provide a hourly report to the requestor of the steps taken and to be taken to resolve the request, the progress to correct, and the estimated time of correction until the request is resolved; and, (d) every [Time Duration], provide increasing levels of technical expertise and Service Provider management involvement in finding a solution to the request until it has been resolved.

c) <u>Problem Severity Levels 3 and 4 Response and Resolution</u>. For Technical Support requests not made by telephone, within the Request Response Time of such a request, Service Provider shall confirm to the requestor receipt of the request by Service Provider. If a Problem Severity Level 3 or 4 request cannot be corrected to the reasonable satisfaction of the requestor within the Request Resolution Time after the requestor makes the initial request for Technical Support, at the sole election of requestor: (a) Service Provider will work continuously to resolve the request; or, (b) requestor and Service Provider will mutually agree upon a schedule within which to resolve the request.

Technical Support Problem Severity Levels

This section corresponds to the preceding section and describes problem severity levels as well as response and resolution times. As with the preceding section, this section is only an example and will likely require significant modification to meet your specific needs.

a) Problem Severity Level 1.

    1) Description. This Problem Severity Level is associated with: (a) Services, as a whole, are non-functional or are not accessible; (b) unauthorized exposure of all of part of Subscriber Data; or, (c) loss or corruption of all or part of Subscriber Data.

    2) Request Response Time. 30 minutes.

    3) Request Resolution Time. 2 hours.

b) Problem Severity Level 2.

    1) Description. This Problem Severity Level is associated with significant and / or ongoing interruption of an Authorized User's use of a critical function (as determined by the Authorized User) of the Services and for which no acceptable (as determined by the Authorized User) work-around is available.

    2) Request Response Time. 1 hour.

    3) Request Resolution Time. 4 hours.

c) Problem Severity Level 3.

    1) Description. This Problem Severity Level is associated with: (a) minor and / or limited interruption of an Authorized User's use of a non-critical function (as determined by the Authorized User) of the Services; or, (b) problems which are not included in Problem Severity Levels 1 or 2.

    2) Request Response Time. 8 hours.

    3) Request Resolution Time. 24 hours.

d) Problem Severity Level 4.

    1) Description. This Problem Severity Level is associated with: (a) general questions pertaining to the Services; or, (b) problems which are not included in Problem Severity Levels 1, 2, or 3.

    2) Request Response Time. 8 hours.

    3) Request Resolution Time. 48 hours.

Customization / Integration Services

Describe all customization / integration services, if any, to be provided by the service provider to enable productive use of the services.

Training Services

Describe all training services, if any, to be provided by the service provider. Include any type of training or method of delivery, including documentation or other materials, web-based or computer-based, instructor-led, train-the-trainer, etc.

Service Levels

The following service levels included in this example Exhibit A are only representative. You will likely need to modify them and add other service levels based on the SaaS you're subscribing to as well as your specific needs. Each of the representative service levels consist of the following elements: definitions, service level standard, calculation, performance credit, and example calculation.

Note that the service level standards are set at 100% (excluding any stipulated exceptions, such as a maintenance window), but that doesn't mean a performance credit (i.e., liquidated damages) kicks in if the service provider misses 100%. As explained under the *Failure to Meet Service Level Standards* provision, the point of a 100% service level standard is to signify what you're paying for. You're not paying for the service provider to perform at 95% or some other level of diminished performance. You contracted for and are paying for 100% performance. Again, while that is the expectation, performance credits don't kick in until some threshold lower than 100% is reached. When considering additional service levels, think of what it is you're paying for. Assume you want, and the service provider has agreed, for each technical support telephone call to be answered in 3-seconds or less. That's what you contracted for and that's what you'll be paying for. Thus, your service level standard should be "100% of all technical support telephone calls for the reporting period shall be answered in 3-seconds or less." Then the threshold for a performance credit must be set. As an example, assume you set the threshold at 98%. That means a performance credit *is not* due if the service provider performs better than 98% but a performance credit *is* due if the service provider performs at 98% or below. Some service providers are unfamiliar with a 100% service level standard, so you may need to explain it two or six or more times, but it's worth repeating: you're paying for 100% performance and that's what the service level standards should reflect.

If, for whatever reason, a 100% service level standard cannot be negotiated with a service provider, consider that the standard for the service provider should be higher than the standard for your internal, on-premises service levels. For example, if your IT department has a 99.5% availability service level, you might fall into the trap of agreeing to the same 99.5% availability service level for a service provider. It sounds reasonable to hold a service provider to the same level as an internal IT department and maybe even unreasonable to hold the service provider to a higher level. However, before making that determination of reasonableness, it's necessary to fully understand what the service level is measuring. For example, with an availability service level, it's very common for a service provider to measure only "back-end" processing and exclude the subscriber's connection. Sometimes service providers will exclude short periods of unavailability; for example, the service must be down for at least fifteen minutes before the unavailability clock starts ticking. An internal IT department likely doesn't have those types of exceptions. Thus, a 99.5% availability service level standard for an internal IT department might translate to a 99.9% standard for a service provider.

The calculation of a service level needs to be exactly that: a mathematical expression with, as appropriate, constants, variables, and operators. Define constants and variables to simplify and clarify the calculation. If the calculation is filled with words (qualitative) versus a mathematical expression (quantitative), you'll likely have problems measuring the service level in the future because of disagreements or confusion over interpretation of the words. Regarding the reporting period over which a service level is calculated: you should ensure that service levels aren't measured over a long period of time, which has the effect of diluting non-performance by averaging it over time. Other than in a few cases such as measuring satisfaction, the monthly measurement of service levels is reasonable and appropriate.

In lieu of a monetary performance credit, a service provider may suggest providing additional days of service as remedy for missed service levels. That may sound reasonable, but, in a way, it's almost the same as agreeing to more days of poor performance—stick to monetary credits.

As painful as it'll be, you absolutely need to develop and include example calculations for each and every service level. Not only does an example calculation serve the important purpose of providing guidance on interpreting a service level, it will actually prove out whether your calculation makes sense or not and it will point out flaws. It's helpful to develop an example calculation where a performance credit is due and one where a performance credit is not due. You don't need to include both examples within the Exhibit A, but you'll know that your calculation works.

Availability Service Level

This service level represents the availability of the service, less any permitted downtime.

1) Definitions.

   (a) "Actual Uptime" shall mean the total minutes in the reporting month that the Services were actually available to Authorized Users for normal use.

   (b) "Maintenance Window" shall mean the total minutes in the reporting month represented by the following day(s) and time(s) during which Service Provider shall maintain the Services: [Day(s) and Time(s)].

   (c) "Scheduled Downtime" shall mean the total minutes in the reporting month represented by the Maintenance Window.

(d) "Scheduled Uptime" shall mean the total minutes in the reporting month less the total minutes represented by the Scheduled Downtime.

2) Service Level Standard. Services will be available to Authorized Users for normal use 100% of the Scheduled Uptime.

3) Calculation. (Actual Uptime / Scheduled Uptime) * 100 = Percentage Uptime (as calculated by rounding to the second decimal point)

4) Performance Credit.

(a) Where Percentage Uptime is greater than 99.98%, no Performance Credit will be due to Subscriber.

(b) Where Percentage Uptime is equal to or less than 99.98%, Subscriber shall be due a Performance Credit in the amount of 10% of the Services Fees (as calculated on a monthly basis for the reporting month) for each full 1% reduction in Percentage Uptime.

5) Example Calculation.

(a) Assuming reporting month is February 2012 (41,760 minutes).

(b) Assuming a Maintenance Window of Sundays from Midnight to 4:00 a.m. Eastern Standard Time (equals Scheduled Downtime of 960 minutes).

(c) Scheduled Uptime equals 40,800 minutes (total minutes of 41,760 in February 2012 less 960 minutes of Scheduled Downtime).

(d) Assuming Actual Uptime of 40,000 minutes. A Percentage Uptime is calculated as follows: (40,000 / 40,800) *100 = 98.04%.

(e) The threshold of 99.99% less the Percentage Uptime of 98.04% = 1.95%.

(f) The difference is greater than a 1% reduction but is less than a 2% reduction; therefore, Subscriber is due 10% of the Services Fees as a Performance Credit.

Services Response Time Service Level

This service level represents the response time of the services. The performance credit is set to 95% versus a higher percentage to acknowledge that there is some potential for Internet latency—the delta between 95% and 100% represents a reasonable "fudge factor" for the benefit of the service provider.

1) Definition(s).

    (a) "Response Time" shall mean the interval of time from when an Authorized User requests, via the Services, a Transaction to when visual confirmation of Transaction completion is received by the Authorized User. For example, Response Time includes the period of time representing the point at which an Authorized User enters and submits data to the Services and the Services display a message to the Authorized User that the data has been saved.

    (b) "Total Transactions" shall mean the total of Transactions occurring in the reporting month.

    (c) "Transaction" or "Transactions" shall mean Services web page loads, Services web page displays, and Authorized User Services requests.

2) Service Level Standard. Transactions will have a Response Time of 1 second or less 100% of the time each reporting month during the periods for which the Services are available.

3) Calculation. ((Total Transactions – Total Transactions failing Standard) / Total Transactions) * 100 = Percentage Response Time (as calculated by rounding to the second decimal point).

4) Performance Credit.

    (a) Where Percentage Response Time is greater than 95.00%, no Performance Credit will be due to Subscriber.

    (b) Where Percentage Response Time is equal to or less than 95.00%, Subscriber shall be due a Performance Credit in the amount of 1% of the Services Fees (as calculated on a monthly basis for the reporting month) for each full 1% reduction in Percentage Response Time.

5) Example Calculation.

(a) Total Transactions during the reporting month equal 42,078.

(b) Total Transactions failing the Standard of 100% equal 2,163.

(c) Percentage Response Time is calculated as follows: ((42,078 – 2,163) / 42,078) * 100 = 94.86%

(d) The threshold of 95.01% less the Percentage Response Time of 94.86% = .15%. The difference is less than a 1% reduction; therefore, Subscriber is not due a Performance Credit.

Technical Support Problem Response Service Level

This service level measures the problem response times for the technical support described in the *Technical Support Description* section and at the problem severity levels described in the *Technical Support Problem Severity Levels* section. The calculation is conducted for each problem severity level.

1) Definition. "Total Problems" shall mean the total of problems occurring in the reporting month.

2) Service Level Standard. Problems shall be confirmed as received by Service Provider 100% of the time each reporting month, in accordance with the Request Response Time associated with the Problem Severity Level.

3) Calculation. ((Total Problems – Total Problems failing Standard) / Total Problems) * 100 = Percentage Problem Response (as calculated by rounding to the second decimal point). Note: This Calculation must be completed for each Problem Severity Level.

4) Performance Credit.

(a) Problem Severity Level 1 – 2.

(1) Where Percentage Problem Response is greater than 99.00%, no Performance Credit will be due to Subscriber.

(2) Where Percentage Problem Response is equal to or less than 99.00%, Subscriber shall be due a Performance Credit in the amount of 1% of the Services Fees (as calculated on a monthly basis for the reporting month) for each full 1% reduction in Percentage Problem Response.

(b) Problem Severity Level 3 – 4.

(1) Where Percentage Problem Response is greater than 90.00%, no Performance Credit will be due to Subscriber.

(2) Where Percentage Problem Response is equal to or less than 90.00%, Subscriber shall be due a Performance Credit in the amount of .5% of the Services Fees (as calculated on a monthly basis for the reporting month) for each full 1% reduction in Percentage Problem Response.

5) Example Calculation (Using Problem Severity Level 1 – 2).

(a) Total Problems during the reporting month equal 68.

(b) Total Problems failing the Standard of 100% equal 3.

(c) Percentage Problem Response is calculated as follows: $((68 - 3) / 68) * 100 = 95.59\%$

(d) The threshold of 99.01% less the Percentage Problem Response of 95.59% = 3.42%. The difference is greater than a 3% reduction but is less than a 4% reduction; therefore, Subscriber is due 3% of the Services Fees as a Performance Credit.

Technical Support Problem Resolution Service Level

This service level measures the problem resolution times for the technical support described in the *Technical Support Description* section and at the problem severity levels described in the *Technical Support Problem Severity Levels* section. The calculation is conducted for each problem severity level.

1) <u>Definition</u>. "Total Problems" shall mean the total of problems occurring in the reporting month.

2) <u>Service Level Standard</u>. Problems shall be resolved by Service Provider 100% of the time each reporting month, in accordance with the Request Resolution Time associated with the Problem Severity Level.

3) <u>Calculation</u>. ((Total Problems – Total Problems failing Standard) / Total Problems) * 100 = Percentage Problem Resolution (as calculated by rounding to the second decimal point). Note: This Calculation must be completed for each Problem Severity Level.

4) <u>Performance Credit</u>.

   (a) <u>Problem Severity Level 1 – 2</u>.

      (1) Where Percentage Problem Resolution is greater than 99.00%, no Performance Credit will be due to Subscriber.

      (2) Where Percentage Problem Resolution is equal to or less than 99.00%, Subscriber shall be due a Performance Credit in the amount of 5% of the Services Fees (as calculated on a monthly basis for the reporting month) for each full 1% reduction in Percentage Problem Resolution.

   (b) <u>Problem Severity Level 3 – 4</u>.

      (1) Where Percentage Problem Resolution is greater than 90.00%, no Performance Credit will be due to Subscriber.

      (2) Where Percentage Problem Resolution is equal to or less than 90.00%, Subscriber shall be due a Performance Credit in the amount of 1% of the Services Fees (as calculated on a monthly basis for the reporting month) for each full 1% reduction in Percentage Problem Resolution.

5) <u>Example Calculation (Using Problem Severity Level 3 – 4)</u>.

   (a) Total Problems during the reporting month equal 17.

   (b) Total Problems failing the Standard of 100% equal 2.

   (c) Percentage Problem Resolution is calculated as follows: ((17 – 2) / 17) * 100 = 88.24%

(d) The threshold of 90.01% less the Percentage Problem Resolution of 88.24% = 1.77%. The difference is greater than a 1% reduction but is less than a 2% reduction; therefore, Subscriber is due 1% of the Services Fees as a Performance Credit.

Subscriber Satisfaction Survey Service Level

This service level represents the satisfaction of users, performed on an annual basis, relating to any element of the services that the parties desire to measure.

1) Definition. "Total Responses" shall mean the total responses from Authorized Users to the annual Subscriber satisfaction survey.

2) Service Level Standard. Authorized Users as identified by Subscriber and as surveyed on an annual basis, shall be completely (100%) satisfied with the Services.

3) Calculation. ((Total Responses – Total Responses failing Standard) / Total Responses) * 100 = Percentage Subscriber Satisfaction (as calculated by rounding to the second decimal point).

4) Performance Credit.

(a) Where Percentage Subscriber Satisfaction is greater than 90.00%, no Performance Credit will be due to Subscriber.

(b) Where Percentage Subscriber Satisfaction is equal to or less than 90.00%, Subscriber shall be due a Performance Credit in the amount of 1% of the Services Fees (as calculated on a monthly basis for the reporting month) for each full 1% reduction in Percentage Subscriber Satisfaction.

5) Example Calculation.

(a) Total Responses for the annual satisfaction survey equal 1,277.

(b) Total Responses failing the Standard of 100% equal 40.

(c) Percentage Subscriber Satisfaction is calculated as follows: ((1,277 – 40) / 1,277) * 100 = 96.86%.

(d) The Percentage Subscriber Satisfaction of 96.86% exceeds the threshold of 90.01%; therefore, Subscriber is not due a Performance Credit.

Appendix I ~ SaaS Agreement

The SaaS Agreement included in this appendix can be downloaded without charge in its most current electronic, editable form at www.stephenguth.com. The SaaS Agreement does not constitute, or substitute for, legal advice. The SaaS Agreement is provided "AS IS" without warranty of any kind. ALL EXPRESS OR IMPLIED REPRESENTATIONS AND WARRANTIES, INCLUDING ANY IMPLIED WARRANTY OF MERCHANTABILITY, FITNESS FOR PARTICULAR PURPOSE, OR NON-INFRINGEMENT, ARE HEREBY EXCLUDED. THE AUTHOR SHALL NOT BE LIABLE FOR ANY DAMAGES ARISING OUT OF OR SUFFERED AS A RESULT OF THE USE OF THIS BOOK OR THE INCLUDED SAAS AGREEMENT.

MASTER SOFTWARE AS A SERVICE AGREEMENT

This agreement ("Agreement") is entered into, to be effective as of [Effective Date] ("Effective Date"), by and between **[SUBSCRIBER NAME]** located at [Subscriber Address] ("Subscriber") and **[SERVICE PROVIDER NAME]** located at [Service Provider Address] ("Service Provider").

RECITALS

WHEREAS, Subscriber requires third-party hosted "software as a service" (the "Services," as further described herein) with respect to certain of its information technology needs;

WHEREAS, Subscriber requested a proposal from Service Provider for such Services;

WHEREAS, Service Provider has experience and expertise in the business of providing the Services;

WHEREAS, Service Provider submitted a proposal to Subscriber to perform such Services on behalf of Subscriber;

WHEREAS, based on Service Provider's superior knowledge and experience relating to such Services, Subscriber has selected Service Provider to provide and manage the Services;

WHEREAS, Service Provider wishes to perform the Services and acknowledges that the successful performance of the Services and the security and availability of Subscriber's data ("Subscriber Data," as further described herein) are critical to the operation of Subscriber's business; and,

WHEREAS, Service Provider has agreed to provide the Services to Subscriber, all on the terms and conditions set forth herein.

NOW, THEREFORE, in consideration of the mutual covenants and representations set forth in this Agreement, the parties hereby agree as follows:

1.   The Services. This Agreement sets forth the terms and conditions under which Service Provider agrees to license to Subscriber certain hosted software and provide all other services necessary for productive use of such software including customization / integration, user identification and password change management, data import / export, monitoring, technical support, maintenance, training, backup and recovery, and change management (the "Services") as further set forth on an Exhibit A (sequentially numbered) in the form of the Exhibit A attached hereto or in other statements of services containing substantially similar information and identified as an Exhibit A. The Agreement shall remain in effect unless terminated as provided for herein.

   1.1   Authorized Users; Authorized Uses. Unless otherwise limited on an Exhibit A, Service Provider grants Subscriber a renewable, irrevocable (unless as provided for herein), nonexclusive, royalty-free, and worldwide right for any Subscriber employee, contractor, or agent, or any other individual or entity authorized by Subscriber, (each, an "Authorized User") to access and use the Services. Other than those limitations expressly described in an Exhibit A, Authorized Users will have no other limitations on their access or use of the Services.

   1.2   Acknowledgement of License Grant. For the purposes of 11 U.S.C. § 365(n), the parties acknowledge and agree that this Agreement constitutes a license grant of intellectual property in software form to Subscriber by Service Provider.

1.3 Changes in Number of Authorized Users. The Services are provided on a tiered basis, such tiers as further described in an Exhibit A. Subscriber agrees to license the initial number of Authorized Users described in such Exhibit A (the "Minimum Commitment"). Subscriber is entitled to increase or decrease the number of Authorized Users on an as-requested basis; provided, however, that Subscriber shall maintain the Minimum Commitment unless the parties otherwise agree to adjust the Minimum Commitment. Should Subscriber elect to change the number of Authorized Users, Service Provider shall reduce or increase Authorized Users to the corresponding tier described in the Exhibit A and adjust the prospective Services Fees accordingly no later than five (5) business days from Subscriber's written request.

1.4 Control and Location of Services. The method and means of providing the Services shall be under the exclusive control, management, and supervision of Service Provider, giving due consideration to the requests of Subscriber. Except as otherwise specified in an Exhibit A, the Services (including data storage), shall be provided solely from within the continental United States and on computing and data storage devices residing therein.

1.4.1 Subcontractors. Service Provider shall not enter into any subcontracts for the performance of the Services, or assign or transfer any of its rights or obligations under this Agreement, without Subscriber's prior written consent and any attempt to do so shall be void and without further effect and shall be a material breach of this Agreement. Service Provider's use of subcontractors shall not relieve Service Provider of any of its duties or obligations under this Agreement.

1.4.2 Offensive or Disparaging Content. Where the Services or any web services affiliated with the Services contain offensive content or portray Subscriber in a disparaging way, either as solely determined by Subscriber, Service Provider shall immediately remove the offensive or disparaging content and Subscriber shall have the right, at Subscriber's sole election, to: (a) immediately terminate this Agreement or any Exhibit A corresponding to the offending or disparaging content and be entitled to a return of any prepaid fees, as liquidated damages and not as a penalty; or, (b) obtain or retain, as the case may be, all fees paid or payable for the entire period of the then-current term, as liquidated damages and not as a penalty, associated with any Exhibit A corresponding to the offending or disparaging content.

1.5   Storage.   The Services shall include the applicable allocation of base data storage described in an Exhibit A.   Service Provider shall immediately notify Subscriber when Subscriber has reached eighty percent (80%) of Subscriber's then-current data storage maximum. Within five (5) calendar days of Subscriber's request, Service Provider shall make additional data storage available to Subscriber at the rates described in the Exhibit A.

1.6   Development and Test Environments.   In addition to production use of the Services, Subscriber is entitled to one development and one test environment for use by Authorized Users at no additional charge.   Such non-production environments shall have the same data storage and processing capacities as the production environment.   Service Provider shall cooperate with Subscriber's requests in managing the non-production environments such as refreshing Subscriber Data upon request.

1.7   Documentation.   The documentation for the Services (the "Documentation") will accurately and completely describe the functions and features of the Services, including all subsequent revisions thereto.   The Documentation shall be understandable by a typical end user and shall provide Authorized Users with sufficient instruction such that an Authorized User can become self-reliant with respect to access and use of the Services. Subscriber shall have the right to make any number of additional copies of the Documentation at no additional charge.

1.8 Changes in Functionality. During the term of an Exhibit A, Service Provider shall not reduce or eliminate functionality in the Services. Where Service Provider has reduced or eliminated functionality in the Services, Subscriber, at Subscriber's sole election and in Subscriber's sole determination, shall: (a) have, in addition to any other rights and remedies under this Agreement or at law, the right to immediately terminate this Agreement or the Exhibit A and be entitled to a return of any prepaid fees; or, (b) determine the value of the reduced or eliminated functionality and Service Provider will immediately adjust the Services Fees accordingly on a prospective basis. Where Service Provider has introduced like functionality in other services, Subscriber shall have an additional license and subscription right to use and access the new services, at no additional charge, with the same rights, obligations, and limitations as for the Services. Where Service Provider increases functionality in the Services, such functionality shall be provided to Subscriber without any increase in the Services Fees.

1.9 No Effect of Click-Through Terms and Conditions. Where an Authorized User is required to "click through" or otherwise accept or made subject to any online terms and conditions in accessing or using the Services, such terms and conditions are not binding and shall have no force or effect as to the Services, this Agreement, or the applicable Exhibit A.

2. Service Levels.

2.1 Service Levels; Time is of the Essence. For the term of an Exhibit A, Service Provider shall provide the Services, force majeure events excepted, during the applicable Service Windows and in accordance with the applicable Service Level Standards, each as described in the Exhibit A, time being of the essence.

2.2   Service Level Reporting. On a monthly basis, in arrears and no later than the fifteenth (15th) calendar day of the subsequent month following the reporting month, Service Provider shall provide reports to Subscriber describing the performance of the Services and of Service Provider as compared to the Service Level Standards; provided, however, that the Subscriber Satisfaction Survey Service Level shall be conducted by Service Provider each year on the anniversary of the Effective Date and the results shall be reported to Subscriber by Service Provider no later than the fifteenth (15th) calendar day of the subsequent month following such anniversary date. The reports shall be in a form agreed-to by Subscriber, and, in no case, contain no less than the following information: (a) actual performance compared to the Service Level Standard; (b) the cause or basis for not meeting the Service Level Standard; (c) the specific remedial actions Service Provider has undertaken or will undertake to ensure that the Service Level Standard will be subsequently achieved; and, (d) any Performance Credit due to Subscriber. Service Provider and Subscriber will meet as often as shall be reasonably requested by Subscriber, but no less than monthly, to review the performance of Service Provider as it relates to the Service Levels. Where Service Provider fails to provide a report for a Service Level in the applicable timeframe, the Service Level shall be deemed to be completely failed for the purposes of calculating a Performance Credit. Service Provider shall, without charge, make Subscriber's historical Service Level reports to Subscriber upon request.

2.3   Failure to Meet Service Level Standards. As further described in an Exhibit A, in the event Service Provider does not meet a Service Level Standard, Service Provider shall: (a) owe to Subscriber any applicable Performance Credit, as liquidated damages and not as a penalty; and, (b) use its best efforts to ensure that any unmet Service Level Standard is subsequently met. Notwithstanding the foregoing, Service Provider will use its best efforts to minimize the impact or duration of any outage, interruption, or degradation of Service. In no case shall Subscriber be required to notify Service Provider that a Performance Credit is due as a condition of payment of the same.

2.3.1 Termination for Material and Repeated Failures. Subscriber shall have, in addition to any other rights and remedies under this Agreement or at law, the right to immediately terminate this Agreement or an Exhibit A, and be entitled to a return of any prepaid fees where Service Provider fails to meet any Service Level Standard: (a) to such an extent that the Subscriber's ability, as solely determined by Subscriber, to use the Services is materially disrupted, force majeure events excepted; or, (b) for four (4) months out of any twelve (12) month period.

2.4 Audit of Service Levels. No more than quarterly, Subscriber or Subscriber's agent shall have the right to audit Service Provider's books, records, and measurement and auditing tools to verify Service Level Standard achievement and to determine correct payment of any Performance Credit. Where it is determined that any Performance Credit was due to Subscriber but not paid, Service Provider shall immediately owe to Subscriber the applicable Performance Credit.

3. Support; Maintenance; Additional Services.

3.1 Technical Support. Service Provider shall provide the Technical Support described in an Exhibit A. The Services Fees shall be inclusive of the fees for the Technical Support.

3.2 Maintenance. Service Provider shall provide bug fixes, corrections, modifications, enhancements, upgrades, and new releases to the Services to ensure: (a) the functionality of the Services, as described in the Documentation, is available to Authorized Users; (b) the functionality of the Services in accordance with the representations and warranties set forth herein, including but not limited to, the Services conforming in all material respects to the specifications, functions, descriptions, standards, and criteria set forth in the applicable Exhibit A and the Documentation; (c) the Service Level Standards can be achieved; and, (d) the Services work with the then-current version and the three prior versions of Internet Explorer, Mozilla Firefox, and Google Chrome Internet browsers. The Services Fees shall be inclusive of the fees for maintenance.

3.2.1   Required Notice of Maintenance. Unless as otherwise agreed to by Subscriber on a case-by-case basis, Service Provider shall provide no less than thirty (30) calendar day's prior written notice to Subscriber of all non-emergency maintenance to be performed on the Services, such written notice including a detailed description of all maintenance to be performed. For emergency maintenance, Service Provider shall provide as much prior notice as commercially practicable to Subscriber and shall provide a detailed description of all maintenance performed no greater than one (1) calendar day following the implementation of the emergency maintenance.

3.2.2   Acceptance of Non-Emergency Maintenance. Unless as otherwise agreed to by Subscriber on a case-by-case basis, for non-emergency maintenance, Subscriber shall have a ten (10) business day period to test any maintenance changes prior to Service Provider introducing such maintenance changes into production (the "Maintenance Acceptance Period"). In the event that Subscriber rejects, for good cause, any maintenance changes during the Maintenance Acceptance Period, Service Provider shall not introduce such rejected maintenance changes into production. At the end of the Maintenance Acceptance Period, if Subscriber has not rejected the maintenance changes, the maintenance changes shall be deemed to be accepted by Subscriber and Service Provider shall be entitled to introduce the maintenance changes into production.

3.3 Customization / Integration Services. Service Provider shall provide the Customization / Integration Services, if any, described in an Exhibit A. The Services Fees shall be inclusive of the fees for the Customization / Integration Services.

3.4 Training Services. Service Provider shall provide the Training Services, if any, described in an Exhibit A. The Services Fees shall be inclusive of the fees for the Training Services.

4. Escrow Agreement. At no additional cost to Subscriber, Service Provider agrees to place in escrow with an escrow agent copies of the most current version of the source and object code for the applicable software that is included as a part of the Services as well as all necessary components to ensure proper function of such software including but not limited to any application program interfaces, configuration files, schematics of software components, build instructions, procedural instructions, and other documentation (collectively, the "Software"). The Software shall also include all updates, improvements, and enhancements thereof from time to time developed by Service Provider and which are necessary to internally support the Services for the benefit of Subscriber. Service Provider agrees that upon the occurrence of any event or circumstance which demonstrates with reasonable certainty the inability or unwillingness of Service Provider to fulfill its obligations to Subscriber in providing the Services, as determined solely by Subscriber, Subscriber shall be entitled to obtain the then-current Software from the escrow agent. At the sole election of Subscriber, Subscriber shall have the right to: (a) perform, at Subscriber's cost and no more than annually, via a third-party escrow verification service that is independent of Service Provider and the escrow agent, a verification of Service Provider's compliance with its escrow obligations hereunder including but not limited to a full usability test of the Software; (b) obtain, at no additional cost to Subscriber and no more than annually, the full usability test results of the Software, such test as performed by a third-party

contracted by Service Provider; and, (c) contract with, at Subscriber's cost, a third-party that is independent of Service Provider to perform services relating to the backup and recovery of the Services and / or Subscriber Data. Service Provider agrees to reasonably cooperate with all third-parties contracted by Subscriber for purposes of this provision. Where Subscriber determines, in Subscriber's sole determination, that Service Provider has failed to fulfill its escrow obligations, Subscriber shall, at Subscriber's sole election: (a) have, in addition to any other rights and remedies under this Agreement or at law, the right to immediately terminate this Agreement or the applicable Exhibit A and be entitled to a return of any prepaid fees; and, (b) be due from Service Provider twenty-five percent (25%) of the annualized Services Fees associated with the applicable Exhibit A for the then-current contract year as liquidated damages and not as a penalty.

5. Audit Rights of Service Provider. Service Provider shall have no right to conduct an on-premises audit of Subscriber's compliance with the use of the Services. No more than once annually, Service Provider shall have the right to request from Subscriber its certification of compliance with the permitted number of Authorized Users for an Exhibit A. Where the actual number of users exceeds the permitted number of Authorized Users, Subscriber, at Subscriber's sole election shall, within thirty (30) business days: (a) reduce the actual number of users so as to be in compliance with the permitted number of Authorized Users in which case no additional Services Fees shall be due to Service Provider; or, (b) acquire the appropriate number of Authorized Users at the rate specified in the Exhibit A so as to be in compliance with the permitted number of Authorized Users.

6. Change Control Procedure. Subscriber may, upon written notice, request changes to the scope of the Services under an Exhibit A. If Subscriber requests an increase in the scope, Subscriber shall notify Service Provider, and, not more than five (5) business days (or other mutually agreed upon period) after receiving the request, Service Provider shall notify Subscriber whether or not the change has an associated cost impact. If Subscriber approves, Subscriber shall issue a change control, which will be executed by the Service Provider. Subscriber shall have the right to decrease the scope and the associated fees for an Exhibit A will be reduced accordingly.

7.   Term and Termination; Renewals.

   7.1   Term.   This Agreement is legally binding as of the
         Effective Date and shall continue until terminated as
         provided for herein. Unless this Agreement or an Exhibit
         A is terminated earlier in accordance with the terms set
         forth herein, the term of an Exhibit A (the "Initial Term")
         shall commence on the Start Date and continue until the
         End Date.   Following the Initial Term and unless
         otherwise terminated as provided for in this Agreement,
         an Exhibit A shall automatically renew for successive
         one (1) year terms (each, a "Renewal Term") until such
         time as a party provides the other party with written
         notice of termination; provided, however, that: (a) such
         notice be given no fewer than thirty (30) calendar days
         prior to the last day of the then-current term; and, (b) any
         such termination shall be effective as of the date that
         would have been the first day of the next Renewal Term.

   7.2   Termination for Convenience. Without limiting the right
         of a party to terminate this Agreement or an Exhibit A as
         provided for in this Agreement, a party may terminate
         this Agreement for convenience upon prior written notice
         to the other party provided that there is no Exhibit A then
         in effect.

   7.3   Termination for Cause. Without limiting the right of a
         party to immediately terminate this Agreement or an
         Exhibit A for cause as provided for in this Agreement, if
         either party materially breaches any of its duties or
         obligations hereunder and such breach is not cured, or
         the breaching party is not diligently pursuing a cure to
         the non-breaching party's sole satisfaction, within thirty
         (30) calendar days after written notice of the breach, the
         non-breaching party may terminate this Agreement or an
         Exhibit A for cause as of a date specified in such notice.

   7.4   Payments upon Termination. Upon the termination of
         this Agreement or an Exhibit A, Subscriber shall pay to
         Service Provider all undisputed amounts due and
         payable hereunder, if any, and Service Provider shall
         pay to Subscriber all amounts due and payable

hereunder, such as Performance Credits and prepaid fees, if any.

7.5   Return of Subscriber Data. Upon the termination of this Agreement or an Exhibit A, Service Provider shall, within one (1) business day following the termination of this Agreement or an Exhibit A, provide Subscriber, without charge and without any conditions or contingencies whatsoever (including but not limited to the payment of any fees due to Service Provider), with a final extract of the Subscriber Data in the format specified by Subscriber. Further, Service Provider shall certify to Subscriber the destruction of any Subscriber Data within the possession or control of Service Provider but such destruction shall occur only after the Subscriber Data has been returned to Subscriber. This Section shall survive the termination of this Agreement.

7.6   Renewals. Should the Services continue beyond the then-current Term, the Services Fees for the Renewal Term may be: (a) increased no more than three percent (3%) on an annualized per-user basis where Subscriber has not increased the number of Authorized Users by ten percent (10%) during the then-current Term; or, (b) decreased by no less than three percent (3%) on an annualized per-user basis where Subscriber has increased the number of Authorized Users by ten percent (10%) or greater during the then-current term.

8.   Transition Services. Provided that this Agreement or an Exhibit A has not been terminated by Service Provider due to Subscriber's failure to pay any undisputed amount due Service Provider, Service Provider will provide to Subscriber and / or to the service provider selected by Subscriber (such service provider shall be known as the "Successor Service Provider") assistance reasonably requested by Subscriber to effect the orderly transition of the Services, in whole or in part, to Subscriber or to Successor Service Provider (such assistance shall be known as the "Transition Services") following the termination of this Agreement or an Exhibit A, in whole or in part. The Transition Services shall be provided on a time and materials basis and may include: (a) developing a plan for the orderly transition of the terminated Services from Service Provider to Subscriber or Successor Service Provider; (b) if

required, transferring the Subscriber Data to Successor Service Provider; (c) using commercially reasonable efforts to assist Subscriber in acquiring any necessary rights to legally and physically access and use any third-party technologies and documentation then being used by Service Provider in connection with the Services; (d) using commercially reasonable efforts to make available to Subscriber, pursuant to mutually agreeable terms and conditions, any third-party services then being used by Service Provider in connection with the Services; and, (e) such other activities upon which the parties may agree. Notwithstanding the foregoing, should Subscriber terminate this Agreement or an Exhibit A due to Service Provider's material breach, Subscriber may elect to use the Services for a period of no greater than six (6) months from the date of termination at a reduced rate of twenty (20%) percent off of the then-current Services Fees for the terminated Services. All applicable terms and conditions of this Agreement shall apply to the Transition Services. This Section shall survive the termination of this Agreement.

9.   Fees; Billing. Subscriber shall be responsible for and shall pay to Service Provider the fees as further described in an Exhibit A, subject to the terms and conditions contained in this Agreement and such Exhibit A. Any sum due Service Provider for the Services for which payment is not otherwise specified shall be due and payable thirty (30) business days after receipt by Subscriber of an invoice from Service Provider.

9.1   Billing Procedures. Unless otherwise provided for under an Exhibit A, Service Provider shall bill to Subscriber the sums due pursuant to an Exhibit A by Service Provider's invoice, which shall contain: (a) Subscriber's purchase order number, if any, and Service Provider's invoice number; (b) description of Services for which an amount is due; (c) the fees or portion thereof that are due; (d); taxes, if any; (e); any Performance Credits or other credits; and, (f) total amount due. Service Provider shall forward invoices in hardcopy format to [Subscriber Accounts Payable Address].

9.2   Taxes. Service Provider represents and warrants that it is an independent contractor for purposes of federal, state, and local taxes. Service Provider agrees that Subscriber is not responsible to collect or withhold any such taxes, including income tax withholding and social security contributions, for Service Provider. Any and all taxes, interest, or penalties, including any federal, state, or local withholding or employment taxes, imposed, assessed, or levied as a result of this Agreement shall be paid or withheld by Service Provider.

9.3   Credits. Any amounts due to Subscriber, such as a Performance Credit, from Service Provider may be applied by Subscriber, at the sole election of Subscriber, against any current or future fees due to Service Provider. Any such amounts that are not so applied by Subscriber shall be paid to Subscriber by Service Provider within thirty (30) calendar days following Subscriber's request. This Section shall survive the termination of this Agreement.

9.4   Non-binding Terms. Any terms and conditions included in a Subscriber purchase order or a Service Provider invoice, as the case may be, shall be deemed to be solely for the convenience of the respective party, and no such term or condition shall be binding upon the parties.

9.5   Auditable Records. Service Provider shall maintain accurate records of all fees billable to, and payments made by, Subscriber in a format that will permit audit by Subscriber for a period of no less than three (3) years from when a fee was incurred or a payment was made. The foregoing obligation of Service Provider shall survive the termination of this Agreement. For the term of this Agreement, upon Subscriber's written request, Service Provider shall provide Subscriber with a copy of its annual American Institute of Certified Public Accountants Service Organization Control (SOC) 1 type 2 report and SOC 2 type 2 report (for all Trust Services Principles).

9.6   Billing Reviews by Third-Parties. For purposes of determining the competitiveness and appropriateness of fees charged to Subscriber by Service Provider, Subscriber is entitled to disclose to a third-party this Agreement, any Exhibit A, and any other data pertaining to fees paid or payable by Subscriber to Service Provider.

9.7 No Suspension of Services. Service Provider shall not suspend any part of the Services where: (a) Subscriber is reasonably disputing any amount due to Service Provider; or, (b) any unpaid but undisputed amount due to Service Provider is less than ninety (90) business days in arrears.

10. Representations and Warranties.

10.1 Mutual. Each of Subscriber and Service Provider represent and warrant that:

10.1.1 it is a business duly incorporated, validly existing, and in good standing under the laws of its state of incorporation;

10.1.2 it has all requisite corporate power, financial capacity, and authority to execute, deliver, and perform its obligations under this Agreement;

10.1.3 the execution, delivery, and performance of this Agreement has been duly authorized by it and this Agreement constitutes the legal, valid, and binding agreement of it and is enforceable against it in accordance with its terms, except as the enforceability thereof may be limited by bankruptcy, insolvency, reorganizations, moratoriums, and similar laws affecting creditors' rights generally and by general equitable principles;

10.1.4 it shall comply with all applicable federal, state, local, or other laws and regulations applicable to the performance by it of its obligations under this Agreement and shall obtain all applicable permits and licenses required of it in connection with its obligations under this Agreement; and,

10.1.5 there is no outstanding litigation, arbitrated matter or other dispute to which it is a party which, if decided unfavorably to it, would reasonably be expected to have a potential or actual material adverse effect on its ability to fulfill its obligations under this Agreement.

10.2 <u>By Service Provider</u>. Service Provider represents and warrants that:

10.2.1   it is in the business of providing the Services;

10.2.2   the Services are fit for the ordinary purposes for which they will be used;

10.2.3   it is possessed of superior knowledge with respect to the Services;

10.2.4   it acknowledges that Subscriber is relying on its representation of its experience and expert knowledge, and that any substantial misrepresentation may result in damage to Subscriber;

10.2.5   it knows the particular purpose for which the Services are required by Subscriber;

10.2.6   it is the lawful licensee or owner of the Services (excluding any Subscriber Data therein) and has all the necessary rights in the Services to grant the use of the Services to Subscriber;

10.2.7   the Services and any other work performed by Service Provider hereunder shall not infringe upon any United States or foreign copyright, patent, trade secret, or other proprietary right, or misappropriate any trade secret, of any third-party, and that it has neither assigned nor otherwise entered into an agreement by which it purports to assign or transfer any right, title, or interest to any technology or intellectual property right that would conflict with its obligations under this Agreement;

10.2.8   it shall disclose any third-party (which shall, for purposes of this Agreement, be deemed a subcontractor) whose intellectual property is incorporated into the Services or who is necessary for the performance of the Services and it shall maintain in-force written agreements with such third-party, if any, for the term of the applicable Exhibit A;

10.2.9 it has the expertise to perform the Services in a competent, workmanlike, and professional manner and in accordance with the highest professional standards;

10.2.10 it will use its best efforts to ensure that no computer viruses, malware, or similar items (collectively, a "Virus") are introduced into Subscriber's computing and network environment by the Services, and that, where it transfers a Virus to Subscriber through the Services, it shall reimburse Subscriber the actual cost incurred by Subscriber to remove or recover from the Virus, including the costs of persons employed by Subscriber;

10.2.11 the Services are free of any mechanism which may disable the Services and Service Provider warrants that no loss of Subscriber Data will result from such items if present in the Services;

10.2.12 in the case of Subscriber's reasonable dispute of any Service Provider invoice, it shall not withhold the performance of Services, including, without limitation, access and use of the Services, Technical Support, Maintenance, and extract of Subscriber Data; and,

10.2.13 the Services will conform in all material respects to the specifications, functions, descriptions, standards, and criteria set forth in the applicable Exhibit A and the Documentation.

11.   Subscriber Data.

11.1   Ownership. Subscriber's data ("Subscriber Data," which shall also be known and treated by Service Provider as Confidential Information) shall include: (a) Subscriber's data collected, used, processed, stored, or generated as the result of the use of the Services; and, (b) personally identifiable information ("PII") collected, used, processed, stored, or generated as the result of the use of the Services, including, without limitation, any information that identifies an individual, such as an individual's social security number or other government-issued identification number, date of birth, address, telephone number, biometric data, mother's maiden name, email address, credit card information, or an individual's name in combination with any other of the elements listed herein. Subscriber Data is and shall remain the sole and exclusive property of Subscriber and all right, title, and interest in the same is reserved by Subscriber. This Section shall survive the termination of this Agreement.

11.2   Service Provider Use of Subscriber Data. Service Provider is provided a limited license to Subscriber Data for the sole and exclusive purpose of providing the Services, including a license to collect, process, store, generate, and display Subscriber Data only to the extent necessary in the providing of the Services. Service Provider shall: (a) keep and maintain Subscriber Data in strict confidence, using such degree of care as is appropriate and consistent with its obligations as further described in this Agreement and applicable law to avoid unauthorized access, use, disclosure, or loss; (b) use and disclose Subscriber Data solely and exclusively for the purpose of providing the Services, such use and disclosure being in accordance with this Agreement, the applicable Exhibit A, and applicable law; and, (c) not use, sell, rent, transfer, distribute, or otherwise disclose or make available Subscriber Data for Service Provider's own purposes or for the benefit of anyone other than Subscriber without Subscriber's prior written consent. This Section shall survive the termination of this Agreement.

11.3   Extraction of Subscriber Data. Service Provider shall, within one (1) business day of Subscriber's request, provide Subscriber, without charge and without any conditions or contingencies whatsoever (including but not limited to the payment of any fees due to Service Provider), an extract of the Subscriber Data in the format specified by Subscriber.

11.4   Backup and Recovery of Subscriber Data. As a part of the Services, Service Provider is responsible for maintaining a backup of Subscriber Data and for an orderly and timely recovery of such data in the event that the Services may be interrupted. Unless otherwise described in an Exhibit A, Service Provider shall maintain a contemporaneous backup of Subscriber Data that can be recovered within two (2) hours at any point in time. Additionally, Service Provider shall store a backup of Subscriber Data in an off-site "hardened" facility no less than daily, maintaining the security of Subscriber Data, the security requirements of which are further described herein. Any backups of Subscriber Data shall not be considered in calculating storage used by Subscriber.

11.5   Loss of Data. In the event of any act, error or omission, negligence, misconduct, or breach that compromises or is suspected to compromise the security, confidentiality, or integrity of Subscriber Data or the physical, technical, administrative, or organizational safeguards put in place by Service Provider that relate to the protection of the security, confidentiality, or integrity of Subscriber Data, Service Provider shall, as applicable: (a) notify Subscriber as soon as practicable but no later than twenty-four (24) hours of becoming aware of such occurrence; (b) cooperate with Subscriber in investigating the occurrence, including making available all relevant records, logs, files, data reporting, and other materials required to comply with applicable law or as otherwise required by Subscriber; (c) in the case of PII, at Subscriber's sole election, (i) notify the affected individuals who comprise the PII as soon as practicable but no later than is required to comply with applicable law, or, in the absence of any legally required notification period, within five (5) calendar days of the occurrence; or, (ii) reimburse Subscriber for any costs in notifying the affected individuals; (d) in the case of PII, provide third-party credit and identity monitoring services to each of the affected individuals who comprise the PII for the period required to comply with applicable law, or, in the absence of any legally required monitoring services, for no less than twelve (12) months following the date of notification to such individuals; (e) perform or take any other actions required to comply with applicable law as a result of the occurrence; (f) without limiting Subscriber's obligations of indemnification as further described in this Agreement, indemnify, defend, and hold harmless Subscriber for any and all Claims (as defined herein), including reasonable attorneys' fees, costs, and expenses incidental thereto, which may be suffered by, accrued against, charged to, or recoverable from Subscriber in connection with the occurrence; (g) be responsible for recreating lost Subscriber Data in the manner and on the schedule set by Subscriber without charge to Subscriber; and, (h) provide to Subscriber a detailed plan within ten (10) calendar days of the occurrence describing the measures Service Provider will undertake to prevent a future occurrence. Notification to affected individuals, as described above, shall comply with applicable law, be written in plain language, and contain, at a minimum: name and contact information of Service Provider's representative; a description of the nature of the loss; a list of the types of data involved; the known or approximate date of the loss; how such loss may affect the affected individual; what steps Service Provider has taken to protect the affected individual; what steps the affected individual can take to protect himself or herself; contact information for major credit card reporting agencies; and, information regarding the credit and identity monitoring services to be provided by Service Provider. This Section shall survive the termination of this Agreement.

12.   Non-Disclosure of Confidential Information. The parties acknowledge that each party may be exposed to or acquire communication or data of the other party that is confidential, privileged communication not intended to be disclosed to third parties. The provisions of this Section shall survive the termination of this Agreement.

12.1   Meaning of Confidential Information. For the purposes of this Agreement, the term "Confidential Information" shall mean all information and documentation of a party that: (a) has been marked "confidential" or with words of similar meaning, at the time of disclosure by such party; (b) if disclosed orally or not marked "confidential" or with words of similar meaning, was subsequently summarized in writing by the disclosing party and marked "confidential" or with words of similar meaning; and, (c) should reasonably be recognized as confidential information of the disclosing party. The term "Confidential Information" does not include any information or documentation that was: (a) already in the possession of the receiving party without an obligation of confidentiality; (b) developed independently by the receiving party, as demonstrated by the receiving party, without violating the disclosing party's proprietary rights; (c) obtained from a source other than the disclosing party without an obligation of confidentiality; or, (d) publicly available when received, or thereafter became publicly available (other than through any unauthorized disclosure by, through, or on behalf of, the receiving party). For purposes of this Agreement, in all cases and for all matters, Subscriber Data shall be deemed to be Confidential Information.

12.2   Obligation of Confidentiality. The parties agree to hold all Confidential Information in strict confidence and not to copy, reproduce, sell, transfer, or otherwise dispose of, give or disclose such Confidential Information to third parties other than employees, agents, or subcontractors of a party who have a need to know in connection with this Agreement or to use such Confidential Information for any purposes whatsoever other than the performance of this Agreement. The parties agree to advise and require their respective employees, agents, and subcontractors of their obligations to keep all Confidential Information confidential.

12.3   Cooperation to Prevent Disclosure of Confidential Information. Each party shall use its best efforts to assist the other party in identifying and preventing any unauthorized use or disclosure of any Confidential Information. Without limiting the foregoing, each party shall advise the other party immediately in the event either party learns or has reason to believe that any person who has had access to Confidential Information has violated or intends to violate the terms of this Agreement and each party will cooperate with the other party in seeking injunctive or other equitable relief against any such person.

12.4   Remedies for Breach of Obligation of Confidentiality. Each party acknowledges that breach of its obligation of confidentiality may give rise to irreparable injury to the other party, which damage may be inadequately compensable in the form of monetary damages. Accordingly, a party may seek and obtain injunctive relief against the breach or threatened breach of the foregoing undertakings, in addition to any other legal remedies which may be available, to include, in the case of Subscriber, at the sole election of Subscriber, the immediate termination, without liability to Subscriber, of this Agreement or any Exhibit A corresponding to the breach or threatened breach.

12.5   Surrender of Confidential Information upon Termination. Upon termination of this Agreement or an Exhibit A, in whole or in part, each party shall, within five (5) calendar days from the date of termination, return to the other party any and all Confidential Information received from the other party, or created or received by a party on behalf of the other party, which are in such party's possession, custody, or control; provided, however, that Service Provider shall return Subscriber Data to Subscriber following the timeframe and procedure described further in this Agreement.   Should Service Provider or Subscriber determine that the return of any non-Subscriber Data Confidential Information is not feasible, such party shall destroy the non-Subscriber Data Confidential Information and shall certify the same in writing within five (5) calendar days from the date of termination to the other party.

13.   Data Privacy and Information Security.

13.1   Undertaking by Service Provider.   Without limiting Service Provider's obligation of confidentiality as further described herein, Service Provider shall be responsible for establishing and maintaining a data privacy and information security program, including physical, technical, administrative, and organizational safeguards, that is designed to: (a) ensure the security and confidentiality of the Subscriber Data; (b) protect against any anticipated threats or hazards to the security or integrity of the Subscriber Data; (c) protect against unauthorized disclosure, access to, or use of the Subscriber Data; (d) ensure the proper disposal of Subscriber Data; and, (e) ensure that all employees, agents, and subcontractors of Service Provider, if any, comply with all of the foregoing. In no case shall the safeguards of Service Provider's data privacy and information security program be less stringent than the safeguards used by Subscriber.

13.2   Audit by Service Provider.   No less than annually, Service Provider shall conduct a comprehensive independent third-party audit of its data privacy and information security program and provide such audit findings to Subscriber.

13.3   Right of Audit by Subscriber.   Without limiting any other audit rights of Subscriber, Subscriber shall have the right to review Service Provider's data privacy and information security program prior to the commencement of Services and from time to time during the term of this Agreement. During the providing of the Services, on an ongoing basis from time to time and without notice, Subscriber, at its own expense, shall be entitled to perform, or to have performed, an on-site audit of Service Provider's data privacy and information security program. In lieu of an on-site audit, upon request by Subscriber, Service Provider agrees to complete, within forty-five (45 days) of receipt, an audit questionnaire provided by Subscriber regarding Service Provider's data privacy and information security program.

13.4   Audit Findings.   Service Provider shall implement any required safeguards as identified by Subscriber or by any audit of Service Provider's data privacy and information security program.

13.5 Subscriber's Right to Termination for Deficiencies. Subscriber reserves the right, at its sole election, to immediately terminate this Agreement or an Exhibit A without limitation and without liability if Subscriber reasonably determines that Service Provider fails or has failed to meet its obligations under this Section.

14. Proprietary Rights.

14.1 Pre-existing Materials. Subscriber acknowledges that, in the course of performing the Services, Service Provider may use software and related processes, instructions, methods, and techniques that have been previously developed by Service Provider (collectively, the "Pre-existing Materials," which shall include the Services) and that the same shall remain the sole and exclusive property of Service Provider.

14.2 No License. Except as expressly set forth herein, no license is granted by either party to the other with respect to the Confidential Information or Pre-existing Materials. Nothing in this Agreement shall be construed to grant to either party any ownership or other interest, in the Confidential Information or Pre-existing Materials, except as may be provided under a license specifically applicable to such Confidential Information or Pre-existing Materials.

14.3 The provisions of this Section shall survive the termination of this Agreement.

15. Indemnification; Limitation of Liability; Insurance.

15.1 General Indemnification. Service Provider agrees to indemnify, defend, and hold harmless Subscriber and its officers, directors, agents, and employees (each, an "Indemnitee") from and against any and all liabilities, damages, losses, expenses, claims, demands, suits, fines, or judgments (each, a "Claim," and collectively, the "Claims"), including reasonable attorneys' fees, costs, and expenses incidental thereto, which may be suffered by, incurred by, accrued against, charged to, or recoverable from any Indemnitee, by reason of any

Claim arising out of or relating to any act, error or omission, negligence, or misconduct of Service Provider, its officers, directors, agents, employees, and subcontractors, during the performance of this Agreement, including, without limitation, Claims arising out of or relating to: (a) bodily injury (including death) or damage to tangible personal or real property; (b) any payment required to be paid to subcontractors, if any, of Service Provider; (c) any material misrepresentation or breach of warranty of any representation or warranty set forth in this Agreement; or, (d) any material breach of any covenant set forth in this Agreement; provided, however, that the foregoing indemnity shall not apply to the extent that the applicable Claim resulted from the acts or omissions of an Indemnitee.

15.2   Proprietary Rights Indemnification.   Service Provider agrees to indemnify, defend, and hold harmless Indemnitees from and against any and all Claims, including reasonable attorneys' fees, costs, and expenses incidental thereto, which may be suffered by, incurred by, accrued against, charged to, or recoverable from any Indemnitee, by reason of any Claim arising out of or relating to the Services infringing or misappropriating any United States or foreign patent, copyright, trade secret, trademark, or other proprietary right. In the event that Service Provider is enjoined from providing the Services and such injunction is not dissolved within thirty (30) calendar days, or in the event that Subscriber is adjudged, in any final order of a court of competent jurisdiction from which no appeal is taken, to have infringed upon or misappropriated any patent, copyright, trade secret, trademark, or other proprietary right in the access or use of the Services, then Service Provider shall, at its expense: (a) obtain for Subscriber the right to continue using such Services; (b) replace or modify such Services so that they do not infringe upon or misappropriate such proprietary right and is free to be used by Subscriber; or, (c) in the event that Service Provider is unable or determines, in its reasonable judgment, that it is commercially unreasonable to do either of the aforementioned, Service Provider shall reimburse to Subscriber any prepaid fees and the full cost associated with any Transition Services.

15.3 <u>Indemnification Procedures</u>. Promptly after receipt by Subscriber of a threat, notice, or filing of any Claim against an Indemnitee, Subscriber shall give notice thereof to Service Provider, provided that failure to give or delay in giving such notice shall not relieve Service Provider of any liability it may have to the Indemnitee except to the extent that Service Provider demonstrates that the defense of the Claim is prejudiced thereby. Service Provider shall have sole control of the defense and of all negotiations for settlement of a Claim and Subscriber shall not independently defend or respond to a Claim; <u>provided</u>, <u>however</u>, that: (a) Subscriber may defend or respond to a Claim, at Service Provider's expense, if Subscriber's counsel determines, in its sole discretion, that such defense or response is necessary to preclude a default judgment from being entered against an Indemnitee; and, (b) Subscriber shall have the right, at its own expense, to monitor Service Provider's defense of a Claim. At Service Provider's request, Subscriber shall reasonably cooperate with Service Provider in defending against or settling a Claim; <u>provided</u>, <u>however</u>, that Service Provider shall reimburse Subscriber for all reasonable out-of-pocket costs incurred by Subscriber (including, without limitation, reasonable attorneys' fees and expenses) in providing such cooperation.

15.4 <u>Third-Party Beneficiaries</u>. For the purposes of this Section and Service Provider's obligations hereunder, non-party Indemnitees are third-party beneficiaries of this Agreement in accordance with its terms. Any action or consent taken by Subscriber on its own behalf is binding upon the non-party Indemnitees for the purposes of this Section. Other than as provided for in this Section, this Agreement is for the sole benefit of the signatories hereto and their permitted successors and assigns. Nothing, express or implied, in this Agreement is intended to create or be construed to create any rights of enforcement in any persons or entities who are neither signatories to this Agreement nor non-party Indemnitees.

15.5 Limitation of Liability. NOTWITHSTANDING ANY OTHER PROVISION SET FORTH HEREIN, NEITHER PARTY SHALL BE LIABLE FOR ANY INDIRECT, SPECIAL, AND / OR CONSEQUENTIAL DAMAGES ARISING OUT OF OR IN CONNECTION WITH THIS AGREEMENT; PROVIDED, HOWEVER, THAT THE FOREGOING EXCULPATION OF LIABILITY SHALL NOT APPLY WITH RESPECT TO DAMAGES INCURRED AS A RESULT OF THE GROSS NEGLIGENCE OR WILLFUL MISCONDUCT OF A PARTY. A PARTY SHALL BE LIABLE TO THE OTHER FOR ANY DIRECT DAMAGES ARISING OUT OF OR RELATING TO ITS PERFORMANCE OR FAILURE TO PERFORM UNDER THIS AGREEMENT; PROVIDED, HOWEVER, THAT THE LIABILITY OF A PARTY, WHETHER BASED ON AN ACTION OR CLAIM IN CONTRACT, EQUITY, NEGLIGENCE, TORT, OR OTHERWISE FOR ALL EVENTS, ACTS, OR OMISSIONS UNDER THIS AGREEMENT SHALL NOT EXCEED THE FEES PAID OR PAYABLE UNDER THIS AGREEMENT, AND PROVIDED, FURTHER, THAT THE FOREGOING LIMITATION SHALL NOT APPLY TO: (A) A PARTY'S OBLIGATIONS OF INDEMNIFICATION, AS FURTHER DESCRIBED IN THIS AGREEMENT; (B) DAMAGES CAUSED BY A PARTY'S GROSS NEGLIGENCE OR WILLFUL MISCONDUCT; OR, (C) A PARTY'S BREACH OF ITS OBLIGATIONS OF CONFIDENTIALITY, AS FURTHER DESCRIBED IN THIS AGREEMENT. This Section shall survive the termination of this Agreement.

15.6 Insurance. Service Provider shall, at its own expense, procure and maintain in full force and effect during the term of this Agreement, policies of insurance, of the types and in the minimum amounts as follows, with responsible insurance carriers duly qualified in those states (locations) where the Services are to be performed, covering the operations of Service Provider, pursuant to this Agreement: commercial general liability ($1,000,000 per occurrence, $2,000,000 aggregate); excess liability ($2,000,000 per occurrence, $2,000,000 aggregate); workers' compensation (statutory limits) and employers' liability ($500,000 per accident); and, professional liability ($1,000,000 per occurrence,

$1,000,000 aggregate). Subscriber shall be named as an additional insured in such policies which shall contain standard cross liability clauses. Service Provider shall cause the liability it assumed under this Agreement to be specifically insured under the contractual liability section of the liability insurance policies. The liability policy shall be primary without right of contribution from any insurance by Subscriber. Such policies shall require that Subscriber be given no less than thirty (30) calendar days prior written notice of any cancellation thereof or material change therein. Subscriber shall have the right to request an adjustment of the limits of liability for commercial general liability and professional liability insurance as Service Provider's exposure to Subscriber increases. Service Provider shall provide Subscriber with certificates of insurance evidencing all of the above coverage, including all special requirements specifically noted above, and shall provide Subscriber with certificates of insurance evidencing renewal or substitution of such insurance thirty (30) calendar days prior to the effective date of such renewal or substitution.

16. <u>General</u>.

16.1 <u>Relationship between Subscriber and Service Provider</u>. Service Provider represents and warrants that it is an independent contractor with no authority to contract for Subscriber or in any way to bind or to commit Subscriber to any agreement of any kind or to assume any liabilities of any nature in the name of or on behalf of Subscriber. Under no circumstances shall Service Provider, or any of its staff, if any, hold itself out as or be considered an agent employee, joint venture, or partner of Subscriber. In recognition of Service Provider's status as an independent contractor, Subscriber shall carry no Workers' Compensation insurance or any health or accident insurance to cover Service Provider or Service Provider's agents or staff, if any. Subscriber shall not pay any contributions to Social Security, unemployment insurance, federal or state withholding taxes, any other applicable taxes whether federal, state, or local, nor provide any other contributions or benefits which might be expected in an employer-employee relationship. Neither Service Provider nor its staff, if any, shall be eligible for, participate in, or accrue any direct or indirect benefit under any other compensation, benefit, or pension plan of Subscriber.

16.2   Governing Law. This Agreement shall be governed by and construed in accordance with the laws of the [State Name] and the federal laws of the United States of America. Service Provider hereby consents and submits to the jurisdiction and forum of the state and federal courts in the [State Name] in all questions and controversies arising out of this Agreement.

16.3   Attorneys' Fees and Costs. In any arbitration, litigation, or other proceeding, informal or formal, by which one party either seeks to enforce this Agreement or seeks a declaration of any rights or obligations under this Agreement, the non-prevailing party shall pay the prevailing party's costs and expenses, including but not limited to, reasonable attorneys' fees.

16.4   Compliance with Laws; Subscriber Policies and Procedures. Both parties agree to comply with all applicable federal, state, and local laws, executive orders and regulations issued, where applicable. Service Provider shall comply with Subscriber policies and procedures where the same are posted, conveyed, or otherwise made available to Service Provider.

16.5   Cooperation. Where agreement, approval, acceptance, consent or similar action by either party hereto is required by any provision of this Agreement, such action shall not be unreasonably delayed or withheld. Each party will cooperate with the other by, among other things, making available, as reasonably requested by the other, management decisions, information, approvals, and acceptances in order that each party may properly accomplish its obligations and responsibilities hereunder. Service Provider will cooperate with any Subscriber supplier performing services, and all parties supplying hardware, software, communication services, and other services and products to Subscriber, including, without limitation, the Successor Service Provider. Service Provider agrees to cooperate with such suppliers, and shall not commit or permit any act which may interfere with the performance of services by any such supplier.

16.6   Force Majeure; Excused Performance. Neither party shall be liable for delays or any failure to perform the Services or this Agreement due to causes beyond its reasonable control. Such delays include, but are not limited to, fire, explosion, flood or other natural catastrophe, governmental legislation, acts, orders, or regulation, strikes or labor difficulties, to the extent not occasioned by the fault or negligence of the delayed party. Any such excuse for delay shall last only as long as the event remains beyond the reasonable control of the delayed party. However, the delayed party shall use its best efforts to minimize the delays caused by any such event beyond its reasonable control. Where Service Provider fails to use its best efforts to minimize such delays, the delays shall be included in the determination of Service Level achievement. The delayed party must notify the other party promptly upon the occurrence of any such event, or performance by the delayed party will not be considered excused pursuant to this Section, and inform the other party of its plans to resume performance. A force majeure event does not excuse Service Provider from providing Services and fulfilling its responsibilities relating to the requirements of backup and recovery of Subscriber Data. In no event shall any of the following constitute a force majeure event: (a) failure, inadequate performance, or unavailability of Service Provider's subcontractors, if any; or, (b) configuration changes, other changes, Viruses, or other errors or omissions introduced, or permitted to be introduced, by Service Provider that result in an outage or inability for Subscriber to access or use the Services. Within thirty (30) calendar days following the Effective Date and on an annual basis thereafter until the termination of this Agreement, Service Provider shall provide its then-current business continuity plan ("Business Continuity Plan") to Subscriber upon Subscriber's request. The Business Continuity Plan shall include: (a) Services and Subscriber Data backup and recovery procedures; (b) fail-over procedures; and, (c) how Service Provider will interact with its business continuity suppliers, if any.

Service Provider shall test its Business Continuity Plan on an annual basis until the termination of this Agreement and shall provide the test results to Subscriber upon Subscriber's request.

16.7 <u>Advertising and Publicity</u>. Service Provider shall not refer to Subscriber directly or indirectly in any advertisement, news release, or publication without prior written approval from Subscriber.

16.8 <u>No Waiver</u>. The failure of either party at any time to require performance by the other party of any provision of this Agreement shall in no way affect that party's right to enforce such provisions, nor shall the waiver by either party of any breach of any provision of this Agreement be taken or held to be a waiver of any further breach of the same provision.

16.9 <u>Notices</u>. Any notice given pursuant to this Agreement shall be in writing and shall be given by personal service or by United States certified mail, return receipt requested, postage prepaid to the addresses appearing at the end of this Agreement, or as changed through written notice to the other party. Notice given by personal service shall be deemed effective on the date it is delivered to the addressee, and notice mailed shall be deemed effective on the third day following its placement in the mail addressed to the addressee.

16.10 <u>Assignment of Agreement</u>. This Agreement and the obligations of Service Provider hereunder are personal to Service Provider and its staff. Neither Service Provider nor any successor, receiver, or assignee of Service Provider shall directly or indirectly assign this Agreement or the rights or duties created by this Agreement, whether such assignment is effected in connection with a sale of Service Provider's assets or stock or through merger, an insolvency proceeding or otherwise, without the prior written consent of Subscriber. In the case of an assignment by Service Provider, Service Provider represents and warrants that it has all requisite rights and power to transfer any agreements or other rights with third-parties whose software is incorporated into the Services or who are necessary for the performance and use of the Services. Subscriber, at Subscriber's sole election, may assign any and all of its rights and obligations under this Agreement to any company that succeeds to substantially all of Subscriber's business.

16.11   Counterparts; Facsimile.   This Agreement may be executed in one or more counterparts, each of which shall be deemed an original, but all of which together shall constitute one and the same Agreement.   The parties agree that a facsimile signature may substitute for and have the same legal effect as the original signature.

16.12   Entire Agreement.   This Agreement and its attached exhibits constitute the entire agreement between the parties and supersede any and all previous representations, understandings, or agreements between Subscriber and Service Provider as to the subject matter hereof.   This Agreement may only be amended by an instrument in writing signed by the parties.   This Agreement shall be construed without regard to the party that drafted it.   Any ambiguity shall not be interpreted against either party and shall, instead, be resolved in accordance with other applicable rules concerning the interpretation of contracts.

16.13   Cumulative Remedies.   All rights and remedies of Subscriber herein shall be in addition to all other rights and remedies available at law or in equity, including, without limitation, specific performance against Service Provider for the enforcement of this Agreement, and temporary and permanent injunctive relief.

Executed on the dates set forth below by the undersigned authorized representative of Subscriber and Service Provider to be effective as of the Effective Date.

[SUBSCRIBER NAME] (SUBSCRIBER)

By:
Name:
Title:
Date:

Address for Notice:

[SERVICE PROVIDER NAME] (SERVICE PROVIDER)
By:
Name:
Title:
Date:

Address for Notice:

EXHIBIT A-____

Service Provider's Software as a Service Statement of Services

This Exhibit A - Service Provider's Software as a Service Statement of Services shall be incorporated in and governed by the terms of that certain Master Software as a Service Agreement by and between **[SUBSCRIBER NAME]** ("Subscriber") and **[SERVICE PROVIDER NAME]** ("Service Provider") dated [Effective Date], as amended (the "Agreement"). Unless expressly provided for in this Exhibit A, in the event of a conflict between the provisions contained in the Agreement and those contained in this Exhibit A, the provisions contained in this Exhibit A shall prevail.

Services Description. [Enter a detailed description of the Services that will be provided. As appropriate, documents describing the Services can be "attached hereto and incorporated herein."]

Start Date and End Date. [Indicate the Start Date and End Date of the Services. These dates represent the term of the Services. If the Services are not required until after Customization / Integration Services, Training Services, etc. are completed, be sure to indicate that the Start Date for the Services may be later than the Start Date for, for example, the Customization / Integration Services.]

Authorized Users and Services Fees. [Indicate the initial number of Authorized Users and rates. Additionally, describe "tiers" or numbers and corresponding rates to purchase additional Authorized Users. Be clear as to the type of pricing model; for example, scalable pricing, module pricing, per seat pricing, usage-based pricing. This Agreement assumes a scalable and elastic per-user pricing model. Also include the billing frequency, such as monthly, quarterly, or annually.]

Storage Threshold(s). [Describe the initial data storage provided by the Service Provider and any additional "tiers" of storage.]

Storage Fees. [Describe Storage Fees, if any, for the initial data storage provided by the Service Provider as well as for any additional "tiers" of storage.]

Technical Support Description. [Modify this section as necessary.] Service Provider will provide to Subscriber telephone and email support ("Technical Support") twenty-four (24) hours per day, seven (7) days per week, three-hundred-sixty-five (365) days per year. Technical Support will include any research and resolution activity performed by Service Provider.

a) Request for Technical Support. Authorized Users will make Technical Support requests by calling or emailing Service Provider's Technical Support staff or by submitting a request via Service Provider's customer service web portal. The Technical Support staff shall assign to the request the Problem Severity Level (as defined herein) indicated by the requestor.

b) Problem Severity Levels 1 and 2 Response and Resolution. For Technical Support requests not made by telephone, within the Request Response Time of such a request, Service Provider shall confirm to the requestor receipt of the request by Service Provider. If a Problem Severity Level 1 or 2 request cannot be corrected to the reasonable satisfaction of the requestor within the Request Resolution Time after the requestor makes the initial request for Technical Support, Service Provider will: (a) immediately escalate the request to Service Provider's management; (b) take and continue to take the actions which will most expeditiously resolve the request; (c) provide a hourly report to the requestor of the steps taken and to be taken to resolve the request, the progress to correct, and the estimated time of correction until the request is resolved; and, (d) every [Time Duration], provide increasing levels of technical expertise and Service Provider management involvement in finding a solution to the request until it has been resolved.

c) Problem Severity Levels 3 and 4 Response and Resolution. For Technical Support requests not made by telephone, within the Request Response Time of such a request, Service Provider shall confirm to the requestor receipt of the request by Service Provider. If a Problem Severity Level 3 or 4 request cannot be corrected to the reasonable satisfaction of the requestor within the Request Resolution Time after the requestor makes the initial request for Technical Support, at the sole election of requestor: (a) Service Provider will work continuously to resolve the request; or, (b) requestor and Service Provider will mutually agree upon a schedule within which to resolve the request.

Technical Support Problem Severity Levels

a) Problem Severity Level 1.

1) Description. This Problem Severity Level is associated with: (a) Services, as a whole, are non-functional or are not accessible; (b) unauthorized exposure of all of part of

Subscriber Data; or, (c) loss or corruption of all or part of Subscriber Data.

   2) <u>Request Response Time</u>. 30 minutes.

   3) <u>Request Resolution Time</u>. 2 hours.

b) <u>Problem Severity Level 2</u>.

   1) <u>Description</u>. This Problem Severity Level is associated with significant and / or ongoing interruption of an Authorized User's use of a critical function (as determined by the Authorized User) of the Services and for which no acceptable (as determined by the Authorized User) work-around is available.

   2) <u>Request Response Time</u>. 1 hour.

   3) <u>Request Resolution Time</u>. 4 hours.

c) <u>Problem Severity Level 3</u>.

   1) <u>Description</u>. This Problem Severity Level is associated with: (a) minor and / or limited interruption of an Authorized User's use of a non-critical function (as determined by the Authorized User) of the Services; or, (b) problems which are not included in Problem Severity Levels 1 or 2.

   2) <u>Request Response Time</u>. 8 hours.

   3) <u>Request Resolution Time</u>. 24 hours.

d) <u>Problem Severity Level 4</u>.

   1) <u>Description</u>. This Problem Severity Level is associated with: (a) general questions pertaining to the Services; or, (b) problems which are not included in Problem Severity Levels 1, 2, or 3.

   2) <u>Request Response Time</u>. 8 hours.

   3) <u>Request Resolution Time</u>. 48 hours.

<u>Customization / Integration Services</u>. [Describe all Customization / Integration Services, if any, to be provided by the Service Provider to enable production use of the Services.]

<u>Training Services</u>. [Describe all Training Services, if any, to be provided by the Service Provider. Include any type of training or method of

delivery, including documentation or other materials, web- or computer-based, instructor-led, train-the-trainer, etc.]

Service Levels.

    a)   Availability Service Level.

        1)   Definitions.

            (a) "Actual Uptime" shall mean the total minutes in the reporting month that the Services were actually available to Authorized Users for normal use.

            (b) "Maintenance Window" shall mean the total minutes in the reporting month represented by the following day(s) and time(s) during which Service Provider shall maintain the Services: [Day(s) and Time(s)].

            (c) "Scheduled Downtime" shall mean the total minutes in the reporting month represented by the Maintenance Window.

            (d) "Scheduled Uptime" shall mean the total minutes in the reporting month less the total minutes represented by the Scheduled Downtime.

        2)   Service Level Standard. Services will be available to Authorized Users for normal use 100% of the Scheduled Uptime.

        3)   Calculation. (Actual Uptime / Scheduled Uptime) * 100 = Percentage Uptime (as calculated by rounding to the second decimal point)

        4)   Performance Credit.

            (a) Where Percentage Uptime is greater than 99.98%, no Performance Credit will be due to Subscriber.

            (b) Where Percentage Uptime is equal to or less than 99.98%, Subscriber shall be due a Performance Credit in the amount of 10% of the Services Fees (as calculated on a monthly basis for the reporting month) for each full 1% reduction in Percentage Uptime.

        5)   Example Calculation.

            (a) Assuming reporting month is February 2012 (41,760 minutes).

(b) Assuming a Maintenance Window of Sundays from Midnight to 4:00 a.m. Eastern Standard Time (equals Scheduled Downtime of 960 minutes).

(c) Scheduled Uptime equals 40,800 minutes (total minutes of 41,760 in February 2012 less 960 minutes of Scheduled Downtime).

(d) Assuming Actual Uptime of 40,000 minutes. A Percentage Uptime is calculated as follows: (40,000 / 40,800) *100 = 98.04%.

(e) The threshold of 99.99% less the Percentage Uptime of 98.04% = 1.95%.

(f) The difference is greater than a 1% reduction but is less than a 2% reduction; therefore, Subscriber is due 10% of the Services Fees as a Performance Credit.

b) Services Response Time Service Level.

   1) Definition(s).

     (a) "Response Time" shall mean the interval of time from when an Authorized User requests, via the Services, a Transaction to when visual confirmation of Transaction completion is received by the Authorized User. For example, Response Time includes the period of time representing the point at which an Authorized User enters and submits data to the Services and the Services display a message to the Authorized User that the data has been saved.

     (b) "Total Transactions" shall mean the total of Transactions occurring in the reporting month.

     (c) "Transaction" or "Transactions" shall mean Services web page loads, Services web page displays, and Authorized User Services requests.

   2) Service Level Standard. Transactions will have a Response Time of 1 second or less 100% of the time each reporting month during the periods for which the Services are available.

   3) Calculation. ((Total Transactions – Total Transactions failing Standard) / Total Transactions) * 100 = Percentage Response Time (as calculated by rounding to the second decimal point).

4) Performance Credit.

(a) Where Percentage Response Time is greater than 95.00%, no Performance Credit will be due to Subscriber.

(b) Where Percentage Response Time is equal to or less than 95.00%, Subscriber shall be due a Performance Credit in the amount of 1% of the Services Fees (as calculated on a monthly basis for the reporting month) for each full 1% reduction in Percentage Response Time.

5) Example Calculation.

(a) Total Transactions during the reporting month equal 42,078.

(b) Total Transactions failing the Standard of 100% equal 2,163.

(c) Percentage Response Time is calculated as follows: $((42,078 - 2,163) / 42,078) * 100 = 94.86\%$

(d) The threshold of 95.01% less the Percentage Response Time of 94.86% = .15%. The difference is less than a 1% reduction; therefore, Subscriber is not due a Performance Credit.

c) Technical Support Problem Response Service Level.

1) Definition. "Total Problems" shall mean the total of problems occurring in the reporting month.

2) Service Level Standard. Problems shall be confirmed as received by Service Provider 100% of the time each reporting month, in accordance with the Request Response Time associated with the Problem Severity Level.

3) Calculation. ((Total Problems − Total Problems failing Standard) / Total Problems) * 100 = Percentage Problem Response (as calculated by rounding to the second decimal point). Note: This Calculation must be completed for each Problem Severity Level.

4) Performance Credit.

(a) Problem Severity Level 1 – 2.

(1) Where Percentage Problem Response is greater than 99.00%, no Performance Credit will be due to Subscriber.

(2) Where Percentage Problem Response is equal to or less than 99.00%, Subscriber shall be due a Performance Credit in the amount of 1% of the Services Fees (as calculated on a monthly basis for the reporting month) for each full 1% reduction in Percentage Problem Response.

(b) Problem Severity Level 3 – 4.

(1) Where Percentage Problem Response is greater than 90.00%, no Performance Credit will be due to Subscriber.

(2) Where Percentage Problem Response is equal to or less than 90.00%, Subscriber shall be due a Performance Credit in the amount of .5% of the Services Fees (as calculated on a monthly basis for the reporting month) for each full 1% reduction in Percentage Problem Response.

5) Example Calculation (Using Problem Severity Level 1 – 2).

(a) Total Problems during the reporting month equal 68.

(b) Total Problems failing the Standard of 100% equal 3.

(c) Percentage Problem Response is calculated as follows: $((68 - 3) / 68) * 100 = 95.59\%$

(d) The threshold of 99.01% less the Percentage Problem Response of 95.59% = 3.42%. The difference is greater than a 3% reduction but is less than a 4% reduction; therefore, Subscriber is due 3% of the Services Fees as a Performance Credit.

d) Technical Support Problem Resolution Service Level.

1) Definition. "Total Problems" shall mean the total of problems occurring in the reporting month.

2) Service Level Standard. Problems shall be resolved by Service Provider 100% of the time each reporting month, in accordance with the Request Resolution Time associated with the Problem Severity Level.

3) Calculation. ((Total Problems – Total Problems failing Standard) / Total Problems) * 100 = Percentage Problem

Resolution (as calculated by rounding to the second decimal point). Note: This Calculation must be completed for each Problem Severity Level.

4) Performance Credit.

    (a) Problem Severity Level 1 – 2.

        (1) Where Percentage Problem Resolution is greater than 99.00%, no Performance Credit will be due to Subscriber.

        (2) Where Percentage Problem Resolution is equal to or less than 99.00%, Subscriber shall be due a Performance Credit in the amount of 5% of the Services Fees (as calculated on a monthly basis for the reporting month) for each full 1% reduction in Percentage Problem Resolution.

    (b) Problem Severity Level 3 – 4.

        (1) Where Percentage Problem Resolution is greater than 90.00%, no Performance Credit will be due to Subscriber.

        (2) Where Percentage Problem Resolution is equal to or less than 90.00%, Subscriber shall be due a Performance Credit in the amount of 1% of the Services Fees (as calculated on a monthly basis for the reporting month) for each full 1% reduction in Percentage Problem Resolution.

5) Example Calculation (Using Problem Severity Level 3 – 4).

    (a) Total Problems during the reporting month equal 17.

    (b) Total Problems failing the Standard of 100% equal 2.

    (c) Percentage Problem Resolution is calculated as follows: $((17 - 2) / 17) * 100 = 88.24\%$

    (d) The threshold of 90.01% less the Percentage Problem Resolution of 88.24% = 1.77%. The difference is greater than a 1% reduction but is less than a 2% reduction; therefore, Subscriber is due 1% of the Services Fees as a Performance Credit.

e) Subscriber Satisfaction Survey Service Level. On an annual basis, Subscriber and Service Provider shall each agree on the structure of the Subscriber satisfaction survey, including question format, question composition, number of questions, response scale (such as Likert), and method of surveying (such as telephonic). Unless otherwise agreed to in writing by Subscriber, all Authorized Users shall be solicited by Service Provide to participate in the Subscriber satisfaction survey.

1) Definition. "Total Responses" shall mean the total responses from Authorized Users to the annual Subscriber satisfaction survey.

2) Service Level Standard. Authorized Users as identified by Subscriber and as surveyed on an annual basis, shall be completely (100%) satisfied with the Services.

3) Calculation. ((Total Responses – Total Responses failing Standard) / Total Responses) * 100 = Percentage Subscriber Satisfaction (as calculated by rounding to the second decimal point).

4) Performance Credit.

   (a) Where Percentage Subscriber Satisfaction is greater than 90.00%, no Performance Credit will be due to Subscriber.

   (b) Where Percentage Subscriber Satisfaction is equal to or less than 90.00%, Subscriber shall be due a Performance Credit in the amount of 1% of the Services Fees (as calculated on a monthly basis for the reporting month) for each full 1% reduction in Percentage Subscriber Satisfaction.

5) Example Calculation.

   (a) Total Responses for the annual satisfaction survey equal 1,277.

   (b) Total Responses failing the Standard of 100% equal 40.

   (c) Percentage Subscriber Satisfaction is calculated as follows: ((1,277 – 40) / 1,277) * 100 = 96.86%.

   (d) The Percentage Subscriber Satisfaction of 96.86% exceeds the threshold of 90.01%; therefore, Subscriber is not due a Performance Credit.

Executed on the dates set forth below by the undersigned authorized representative of Subscriber and Service Provider to be effective as of the Start Date.

[SUBSCRIBER NAME] (SUBSCRIBER)
By: For Reference Only
Name: For Reference Only
Title: For Reference Only
Date: For Reference Only

[SERVICE PROVIDER NAME] (SERVICE PROVIDER)

By: For Reference Only
Name: For Reference Only
Title: For Reference Only
Date: For Reference Only

Appendix II ~ Defined Terms

The following terms are defined to have a specific meaning by the SaaS Agreement contained in *Appendix I ~ SaaS Agreement*. In some cases, the meaning of a certain term as defined in this appendix and by the SaaS Agreement may be different from the industry-recognized definition.

Actual Uptime – Component of the Availability Service Level calculation. The total minutes in the reporting month that the Services were actually available to Authorized Users for normal use.

Agreement – The SaaS Agreement executed between the Subscriber and the Service Provider, as well as all exhibits, schedules, and addenda.

Authorized User(s) – Any individual who has the right to access and use the Services.

Availability Service Level – Measures the Service Provider's performance relative to the availability of the Services for the reporting month, excluding the permissible unavailability of the Services as represented by the Scheduled Downtime.

Claims – Collectively refers to those categories of liabilities subject to indemnification.

Confidential Information – Data, information, and communications of the parties not intended to be disclosed to unauthorized third-parties. In the case of Subscriber, Confidential Information includes Subscriber Data.

Customization / Integration Services – The portion of the Services, described in an Exhibit A, related to the customization and / or integration of the Services as required by the Subscriber.

Documentation – The Subscriber- and Authorized User-oriented documentation which describes the then-current functions and features of the Services.

Effective Date – The date that the Agreement was executed by both the Subscriber and the Service Provider, and the date that the Agreement becomes effective.

Indemnitee(s) – Collectively refers to those parties benefiting from the other party's obligation of indemnification.

Initial Term – The initial term of an Exhibit A that commences on the Start Date and continues until the End Date (and which is automatically succeeded by a Renewal Term).

Maintenance Acceptance Period – The period within which the Subscriber is entitled to test Non-Emergency Maintenance. Unless otherwise described in an Exhibit A, the Maintenance Acceptance Period is 10-business days.

Maintenance Window – Component of the Availability Service Level calculation. The total minutes in the reporting month represented by the day(s) and time(s), as agreed upon between the Subscriber and the Service Provider, during which the Service Provider shall maintain the Services.

Minimum Commitment – The initial number of Authorized Users, as described in an Exhibit A, licensed by the Subscriber and which, indirectly, represents an approximate revenue commitment. Unless otherwise adjusted as agreed to by the parties, the Subscriber must maintain the Minimum Commitment for the term of an Exhibit A.

Percentage Problem Resolution – Result of the Technical Support Problem Resolution Service Level calculation. Represents the Service Provider's performance, by Problem Severity Level, relative to resolving Technical Support requests made by Authorized Users in the reporting month.

Percentage Problem Response – Result of the Technical Support Problem Response Service Level calculation. Represents the Service Provider's performance, by Problem Severity Level, relative to responding to Technical Support requests made by Authorized Users in the reporting month.

Percentage Response Time – Result of the Services Response Time Service Level calculation. Represents the Service Provider's performance relative to the Response Time of the Transactions within the reporting month for the Services.

Percentage Subscriber Satisfaction – Result of the Subscriber Satisfaction Survey Service Level calculation. Represents the Service Provider's performance relative to Authorized Users' satisfaction as surveyed on an annual basis.

Percentage Uptime – Result of the Availability Service Level calculation. Represents the Service Provider's performance relative to the availability of the Services for the reporting month.

Performance Credit – The portion of the Services Fee, in the form of liquidated damages, that is due to the Subscriber as a result of a Service Level that does not achieve the required threshold.

PII (personally identifiable information) – A subset of Subscriber Data that identifies an individual, such as an individual's social security number.

Pre-Existing Materials – Materials, such as software, previously developed by the Service Provider and used to deliver or perform the Services. While they can be used by the Subscriber, Pre-Existing Materials remain the sole and exclusive property of the Service Provider.

Problem Severity Level(s) – Used to categorize, based on specified criteria described in an Exhibit A, the severity of Technical Support requests made by Authorized Users. Also describes, by Problem

Severity Level, Request Response Time and Request Resolution Time requirements.

Renewal Term – A 1-year term that automatically follows the Initial Term or a prior Renewal Term of an Exhibit A.

Request Response Time(s) – The specified time, as described in an Exhibit A and categorized by Problem Severity Level, in which the Service Provider must respond to a Technical Support request made by an Authorized User.

Request Resolution Time(s) – The specified time, as described in an Exhibit A and categorized by Problem Severity Level, in which the Service Provider must resolve a Technical Support request made by an Authorized User.

Response Time – Component of the Services Response Time Service Level calculation. The interval of time from when an Authorized User requests, via the Services, a Transaction to when visual confirmation of Transaction completion is received by the Authorized User.

Scheduled Downtime – Component of the Availability Service Level calculation. The total minutes in the reporting month represented by the Maintenance Window

Scheduled Uptime – Component of the Availability Service Level calculation. The total minutes in the reporting month less the total minutes represented by the Scheduled Downtime.

Service Level Standard(s) – Represents the expected standard of performance by the Service Provider for a Service Level.

Service Level(s) – A category of Services measurement, as described in an Exhibit A, to determine the Service Provider's performance relative to the Service Level Standard. Based on the Service Provider's performance for a particular Service Level, the Subscriber may or may not be due a Performance Credit.

Service Provider – The seller entity / licensor, described in the preamble of the Agreement, that will be providing the Services (i.e., SaaS and related services).

Services – Individually and collectively refers to services to be provided by the Service Provider, including the hosted software, customization / integration, user identification and password change management, data import / export, monitoring, technical support, maintenance, training, backup and recovery, and change management as further described in an Exhibit A.

Services Description – A summary description, as described in an Exhibit A, of all elements of the Services.

Services Fees – Fees, described in an Exhibit A, that are specific to Authorized Users for the right to access and use the Services. The SaaS Agreement assumes a scalable and elastic per-user pricing model.

Services Response Time Service Level – Measures the Service Provider's performance relative to the Response Time of the Transactions within the reporting month for the Services.

Software – The software (and all required components) necessary to provide the Services and that is required to be placed into escrow. Subject to certain events, the Subscriber is entitled to obtain the Software from the escrow agent and use the Software in place of the Services.

Storage Fees – Fees, if any, described in an Exhibit A, associated with data storage capacity provided by the Service Provider.

Storage Threshold(s) – The data storage capacity, described in an Exhibit A, necessary to accommodate the storage of Subscriber Data. The description may also include additional tiers of data storage that can be purchased by the Subscriber should the need arise.

Subscriber – The customer entity / licensee entity, described in the preamble of the Agreement, that will be consuming the Services.

Subscriber Data – A subset of Confidential Information that is comprised of Subscriber's data or PII collected, obtained, used in, stored, generated, or produced as the result of the use of the Services.

Subscriber Satisfaction Survey Service Level – Measures the Service Provider's performance relative to Authorized Users' satisfaction as surveyed on an annual basis.

Successor Service Provider – The service provider selected by the Subscriber that will succeed the Service Provider when the Services are terminated or are expiring.

Technical Support – The portion of the Services, described in an Exhibit A, related to the research and resolution of requests for support, as categorized by Problem Severity Level, made by Authorized Users.

Technical Support Problem Resolution Service Level – Measures the Service Provider's performance, by Problem Severity Level, relative to resolving Technical Support requests made by Authorized Users in the reporting month.

Technical Support Problem Response Service Level – Measures the Service Provider's performance, by Problem Severity Level, relative to responding to Technical Support requests made by Authorized Users in the reporting month.

Total Problems – Component of the Technical Support Problem Response Service Level and Technical Support Problem Resolution Service Level calculations. The total of problems occurring in the reporting month.

Total Responses – Component of the Subscriber Satisfaction Survey Service Level calculation.

Total Transactions – Component of the Services Response Time Service Level calculation. The total of Transactions occurring in the reporting month.

Training Services – The portion of the Services, described in an Exhibit A, related to the training needs of Authorized Users to enable their productive use of the Services.

Transaction(s) – Component of the Services Response Time Service Level calculation. Services web page loads, Services web page displays, and Authorized User Services requests

Transition Services – Services to be provided by the Service Provider to effect the orderly transition of terminating or expiring Services to the Successor Service Provider.

Virus – Collectively refers to any type of computer viruses, malware, or similar harmful item.

Index

A

M

N

O

P

R

W